Intrapreneurship

To my children, Talya, a budding enabler
and Gabriel, a change agent,
and to my wife Joey, a real animateur

Intrapreneurship

How to be an enterprising individual in a successful business

Ronnie Lessem

Wildwood House

First published in hardback 1986 by
Gower Publishing Company Limited as *Enterprise Development*

This paperback edition published 1987 by
Wildwood House Limited
Gower House,
Croft Road,
Aldershot,
Hampshire GU11 3HR,
England.

British Library Cataloguing in Publication Data

Lessem, Ronnie
   [Enterprise development]. Intrapreneurship.
   —(Management skills library).
   1. Industrial management—Great Britain—
   Case studies
   I. [Enterprise development]   II. Title
   658'.00941   HD70.G7

   ISBN 0 7045 0577 0

Printed and bound in Great Britain by
Biddles Ltd, Guildford and King's Lynn

Contents

Preface

This book has been written for those of you who want to develop your individuality through business, that is by becoming 'intrapreneurs'.

It is over a year now since my book *Enterprise Development*, on which this paperback version is based, appeared. Before and during this time I have been helping to develop individuality in business, both north and south of the Equator.

In Great Britain, my country of residence, I have been working with medium-sized companies, and with large corporations, to stimulate individuality through intrapreneurship. At ICI (Agriculture) we have worked with research scientists to *develop their business acumen*. At ICI (Paints), we have helped research scientists *identify and develop their individual and innovative role* – be it as inventor, gatekeeper, product champion or project controller – within the innovation process. At British Rail we have *enabled production managers to evolve their roles*, drawing out their business individualities. We have also enabled personnel managers to strengthen their personal vision and influence by building upon their individual and national (Welsh, Scottish, Irish or English) foundations.

In a middle-sized engineering company, we have been developing seven kinds of intrapreneur so as to *enhance the company's ability to adapt to change, and to become more enterprising*. The intrapreneurs on this particular programme are described in Chapter 14.

Intrapreneurship, of course , is not unique to the UK,

though the approach that I have adopted draws on British experience. Compare and contrast this book, for example, with Gifford Pinchot's distinctively American approach to intrapreneuring.[1]

In Africa, I have found several companies with which I have been working particularly receptive. In fact, companies ranging from the mining multinational, Rio Tinto, to the agriculturally based Eastern Highlands Tea Estates — both in Zimbabwe — have responded to 'intrapreneurship' in a distinctive way. For them, it has been an important *vehicle for drawing out the complementary aptitudes of different cultural groupings* within Southern Africa. For although there are no hard-and-fast rules, the Africans were often the 'visionaries' or 'enablers' (new designers), while the Europeans were the 'managers' and 'entrepreneurs'.

Finally, in the UK and in Africa, we have made extensive use of 'intrapreneurship' in education. Firstly, at City University Business School, with my first-year undergraduates in business studies, I use the approach to *help them chart their future vocation*. With my MBA students in London and in Harare, I use it to *help them identify their own potential, and to recognise how it can be harnessed within larger organisations*.

Finally, and interestingly enough, the 'intrapreneurs' portrayed in this book have been used as role models for thousands of women, who have attended 'Finding Your Niche' programmes that we have run in conjunction with the national women's magazine, *Living*. By identifying their individual orientations, the participants have been able to *pinpoint their career focus*, whether in business, in management, in community work or in further education, or in self-development.

Thus the scope for application ranges across north and south, across industry and academia, as well as across individual and organisation. I hope that 'intrapreneurship' can be of some value to you, as you chart your own individual or organisational future.

Ronnie Lessem
June 1987

Reference

1   Pinchot, G., *Intrapreneuring*, Harper & Row 1984.

Acknowledgements

This book would not exist without the intrapreneurs, all of them British, upon whom it is founded. My great thanks to Sir Terence Conran, Mary Quant, Sir John Harvey Jones, Jack Dangoor, Steve Shirley, Nelli Eichner and Anita Roddick, for participating so imaginatively, aesthetically, authoritatively, wilfully, intelligently, enthusiastically, and energetically in this book. Since the original research was done, some of these individuals may have moved on; nevertheless, the thinking in the case studies remains valid.

For the theory behind it I have to thank Kevin Kingsland, Bernard Lievegoed and Reg Revans in particular. Malcolm Stern and Ellen Keeling did me a great service in their editing, and Sue Patience in her typing. Finally, I want to thank this country for providing me, as a colonial emigré, with the opportunity to participate in its business development, alongside my own.

RL

The cast
of characters

Innovator	Sir Terence Conran Chairman, Habitat/ Mothercare	Sir Terence has transformed retailing in the UK through a design- led revolution on the High Street.
New designer	Mary Quant Founder, Mary Quant Ltd.	Mary has, over the past 25 years, become a household name in cosmetics, fashion and soft furnishings.
Leader	Sir John Harvey Jones Chairman, ICI	Sir John, in turning ICI around in three years, has become Britain's archetypal manager of change, and the company's most charismatic leader.

New entrepreneur	Jack Dangoor Founder, Director Advance Technology	Jack has created a computer manufacturing business, with a turnover of many millions, and a staff of seven, in two years.
Change agent	Steve Shirley Founder, Director F International	'Steve' has established a unique organisation — a computer software house, staffed by a panel of 800 women, three-quarters of whom work from home.
Animateur	Nelli Eichner Director, Interlingua (translations/ interpreting)	Nelli is founder and matriarch of an internationally based family business, doing translations and interpreting, and peopled by innumerable nationalities and information technologies.
Adventurer	Anita Roddick Founder, Director, Body Shop	Anita has transformed the cosmetics industry, in eight years, by establishing over 100 franchised outlets for natural skin and hair care products, all over the world.

Part I

The transformation we are experiencing now may well
be more dramatic than any of the preceding ones,
because the rate of change in our age is faster than
ever before, because the changes are more extensive,
involving the entire globe, and because several major
transitions are coinciding . . . As individuals, as a society,
as a civilisation, and as a planetary ecosystem, we are
reaching the turning point.

Fritjof Capra, *The Turning Point*

1 Introduction

> When a man is master of his own sphere, whatever it may be, he has won his degree, he has entered the realm of wisdom.
>
> Henry Ford, *My Life and Years*

Introducing the 'intrapreneur'

This book has been a voyage of discovery. Yet I feel that my voyage has only just begun. Every weekend, when I scan the Sunday papers, the job advertisements seem more intriguing and daunting. As business in the UK leaves the recession behind and communications technology spreads its wings, companies seek a new breed of manager. They seek him here, they seek him there, they seek him almost everywhere. He is required in product development, in systems development, in market development, or in commercial development. I call him the 'intrapreneur'. He is the agent of enterprise development.

The term intrapreneur immediately sets up a creative tension. For 'intra' means 'going within', inside of; 'preneur', from the French 'prendre', means to take, to go out, to undertake. Within this field of tension lies, in fact, not one particular kind of manager, but a whole cast of characters, set on enterprise development. In fact, the intrapreneur is a 'holding category' for seven subsidiaries: the innovator, enabler, leader, entrepreneur, change agent, animateur, and adventurer. How

3

we came to these seven will be revealed in the next chapter. But the reasons why are clear. Firstly, the modern corporation requires a more varied cast of characters than either the traditional manager or entrepreneur. Secondly such a cast, as far as I am concerned, should reinforce, rather than detract from, our individuality. As the Chairman of ICI said to a group of managers in a recent speech, contemporary organisation should serve the individual rather than vice versa.

This book is therefore designed to help managers develop such singular and varied attributes as:

- commercial insight and market awareness
- an ability to work persistently and autonomously
- an innovative and creative mind
- ability to manage and direct change
- organisational capacity and analytical skill
- stamina and staying power
- ability to get on with people at all levels.

(These have been culled from job adverts, in the *Sunday Times,* in the period January to March 1984.)

Where, then, can I begin? Certainly conventional business and management training does not claim to develop more than a small proportion of these attributes. Let me start by reviewing my own educational experiences, and my own route to discovering the intrapreneur.

Re-discovering the entrepreneur

In the summer of 1968 I graduated from Harvard Business School as a 'Master' of Business Administration. I thought that the world was at my feet. I had achieved mastery. In fact, nothing could be further from the truth. Certainly, I had met some amazing people, and gained a modicum of practical knowledge. All in all, it was an exhilarating experience. But I had become, in essence, master of nothing. For true mastery can only be acquired through a rich mixture of knowledge, activity and experience, acquired over an extended period of time. Moreover, if such a healthily varied diet is to be truly assimilated, it has to be made up to suit an individual's metabolism.

Until the 1950s, at least in Great Britain, management was something you did, and not a subject that was taught. In fact, the Victorian entrepreneurs, who spearheaded our industrial revolution, were well known as truly 'self-made men'. They had acquired their knowledge of both technology and of business through personal experience. They had found their own, intensely personal way of mastering business and engineering. In contrast, the business and management schools that grew up, on both sides of the Atlantic, adopted a highly impersonal approach. The management themes and business techniques which were taught were often applied to particular situations, but they were supposed to suit all students. The eventual outcome was a growing outcry[1] particularly in America. The fear was that academia was breeding a select group of business 'analysts', largely out of touch with the more personal qualities possessed by individual business leaders and entrepreneurs.

In fact, it may well be that the business schools had been producing masters of business 'administration', rather than masters of 'business'. As has often been pointed out,[2] two of the most successful industrial nations of recent years, Japan and West Germany, are noted for their lack of business schools.

In the wake of this reaction against 'paralysis by analysis' has come a reinstatement of the 'entrepreneur'. Suddenly the 'entrepreneurial manager' has been discovered or rediscovered. Major corporations, particularly in fast growing industries, are calling for thrusting, risk-taking business managers with 'commercial' and 'entrepreneurial flair'. In effect, we have come full circle, once more to applaud the very qualities which, until very recently, had been disregarded.

Yet history never repeats itself. Instead, it moves relentlessly forward towards an onrushing, but unknown future. In our haste to welcome the entrepreneur back into our midst, we have made the singular mistake of indulging in 'hero worship'. Having worked, over the past five years, with more than a thousand individual entrepreneurs, to help them set up in business, I have become acutely aware of the misplaced adulation. All too many administrators have told me how marvellous these entrepreneurs must be, but how distant from themselves and their organisations. In other words, managers and entrepreneurs still remain divided – now by adulation rather than denigration. But we are beginning to find a way of creating genuine dialogue between the two. In fact, the 'intrapreneur' is paving the way.

Developing a new management concept

When the British journalist, Norman Macrae, introduced 'The Coming Entrepreneurial Revolution',[3] readers provided much applause and little action. Macrae coined the term 'intrapreneur', and applied it to those managers, professionals and artisans of the future, who would set up new and small businesses within old and existing organisations.

Whereas in 1976 Macrae's article was generally 'seen', but not 'heard', today the situation is different. The period of intense rationalisation in the late seventies and early eighties has led to large scale redundancies. A significant number of the technical, managerial and professional people, leaving the managed organisation, set up their own new business instead of seeking re-employment. Some of those self-employed continued to remain in contact with their previous companies, through sub-contracting, part-time consultancies, 'networking', or even a managed 'buy out'.

At the same time, as I have already said, there has been a call for more entrepreneurism within the major corporations. So the juxtaposition of change within and change without is creating a new business culture. The result is that Macrae's prophetic words have come home to roost, not in the mid-seventies, but in the mid-eighties.

And yet, Macrae got his 'intrapreneurial' concept wrong, at least for our time. Contemporary developments in lifestyle, technology and organisation are calling for a much more robust and varied concept of 'intrapreneur' than the one Macrae created. For Macrae, the intrapreneur was merely an entrepreneur within an existing organisation. For me, he or she is qualitatively different, and essentially more complex and varied than his/her entrepreneurial counterpart.

The new intrapreneur

For me, the term 'intrapreneur' is significant in two ways. Firstly, it cuts across the division between management and enterprise. But secondly, it forms a bridge between enterprise and development. Enterprise emerges from the old, instinctive world of small business. Development is part of the new world, one in which the conscious development of people and organisations have a part to play. In the old world, people believe that entrepreneurs are born, not made. In the new world, the one I inhabit, we believe that intrapreneurial abilities can be developed. Hence enterprise development is of concern to both the new manager and the new educator. My objective, in this book, is to create a healthy dialogue between them. How can this be achieved?

The first is to recognise that both have a point so that businesses must be considered from lofty heights and from the ground floor. This is why this book concerns itself with both vision and action, as well as the many steps in between personal and business development. The second is to develop a sufficiently varied number of intrapreneurial types, to match the individual and economic variety that characterises our times. I have identified seven such archetypes, drawing upon a particular approach to business and personality called spectrum theory (see Chapter 2).

The business development archetypes

What I want to do now is to break down the single division between manager and entrepreneur, and to replace it with several 'archetypes'. Each operates successfully within his personal and business domains. The basis for mastery lies in connecting the two. The seven characters that you will meet have each succeeded in a different way with a different personality, and in a different field. Across all seven fields and personalities the full range of intrapreneurial potential is represented. This is portrayed in Table 1.1 and descriptions below.

Table 1.1
Intrapreneurial types

Type	Representative	Company	Industry
Innovator	Sir Terence Conran	Habitat-Mothercare	Retailing
Designer	Mary Quant	Mary Quant Ltd.	Design
Leader	Sir John Harvey Jones	ICI	Manufacturing
Entrepreneur	Jack Dangoor	Advance Technology	Computing
Change agent	Steve Shirley	F International	Computer services
Animateur	Nelli Eichner	Interlingua	Communications
Adventurer	Anita Roddick	Body Shop	Health Care

The INNOVATOR, Sir Terence Conran, has transformed a whole industry. He has turned an original vision into creative action. Conran follows in the footsteps of such innovators as Alfred Nobel, Henry Ford, and now Clive Sinclair, who all transformed their industries. Conran began in home furnishings and has since expanded into household accessories, books and clothing. Terence's personality is charismatic, and he has a captivating vision.

The DESIGNER, Mary Quant, has displayed remarkable design ability and awareness in harnessing the potential of markets which had gone previously undiscovered. In fields as wide ranging as ladies fashions and hairstyling, women's cosmetics and home decorations, she has become known to 90 per cent of the women in this country. Mary has

intuitively sensed what people have wanted, and, in association with innumerable manufacturers and distributors has
developed the right products at the right time. Mary's personality is magnetic, and she has compelling insight.

The LEADER, Sir John Harvey Jones, in a short span of
time, has infused ICI with authority and direction. Striving
for excellence, in many fields of endeavour, he has completely
re-structured his Board, so that it now functions as an integrated whole. Profitability and productivity, at ICI, has
increased dramatically, and the whole image of the company
has changed. This has arisen through the sheer force of John's
authoritative personality. He has limitless capacity to provide
direction.

The NEW ENTREPRENEUR, Jack Dangoor, is an intriguing
mixture of old fashioned 'jungle fighter' and modern 'gamesman'.[4] In an extremely competitive market, Jack has created
a highly successful business, in virtually no time, through
a mixture of old fashioned dealing and new fangled enterprise.
Unlike the entrepreneur of old, who struck out completely
on his own, Jack Dangoor has collaborated with three major
business establishments, to create Advance Technology. Jack
is a dynamic personality, with tremendous flair.

The CHANGE AGENT, Steve Shirley, has created a business
out of a social cause. She has freed women, including herself,
from having to choose between home and career, by providing them with the opportunity to pursue both. Through F
International she has established the kind of flexible structures
and systems that enable 800 women, as systems analysts
and computer programmers, to work in amenable locations
on chosen projects. Steve is an idealist who has institutionalised (F)lexibility.

The ANIMATEUR, a term borrowed from the French, was
originally someone who brought life to the community, or
neighbourhood. I have applied the term to business organisation, drawing out the recent focus on organisational climate,
culture, myth and ritual. Nelli Eichner, founder of Interlingua,
developed an enterprise not so much to make money, but
to apply her love of languages in a field which could engage
her family. In the process she created a 'family of nations'
for which she is both story maker and story teller. Nelli

is a charming personality, with boundless enthusiasm.

The ADVENTURER, Anita Roddick, has travelled round the world, like the great explorers of old, not to discover new territory, but to uncover natural products. In creating 'Bódyshop' she has combined a love of nature with a restless physical energy, to emerge with a franchised chain of hair and skin care products and outlets. As she continues to travel to distant places, picking up ever more natural ingredients, her life and business becomes a continuous adventure. Anita is an extraordinarily energetic person, who loves physically venturing into the unknown.

Achieving mastery in business

Historically, achieving mastery, whether in management or in mountaineering, has been an active process. It was left to poets and novelists to discover the inner meaning of outside achievement. It is my belief, reinforced by my experiences of masters of change, that mastery can be consciously developed, both inwardly – through self-development, as well as outwardly – through business development. Because most business books have concentrated on the second, I want to redress the balance, by paying at least as much attention to the first.

The inward approach to mastery, which I shall be describing in the next chapter, involves not navel gazing, nor even psychoanalysis, but a process of honest communication with oneself and with others. The object of such communication is gradually to open ourselves, via others, to aspects of our personality which have remained hitherto concealed. Correspondingly, the outward approach involves undergoing activities and experiences with draw out qualities hitherto untried and tested. To achieve genuine mastery we need to be able to journey inward, and outward, at one and the same time. Personal and business development needs to go hand in hand. I have therefore tried, in this book, to provide case histories of intrapreneurs, in which both the inward and outward journeys are clearly evident.

The structure of the book

Part I of this book introduces you to 'spectrum theory'. Not only is it the theory that underlies the seven intrapreneurial 'types', but it also provides a basis for developing personal and business mastery.

In Part II I introduce you to the intrapreneurs, or 'masters of change'. I ensure that each intrapreneurial 'archetype' not only tells his or her tale, but is also very briefly set in context within the relevant business and management theory. These references are brief, as this book is not intended to be heavily laden with conventional theory.

In Part III I have drawn out the implications for the training of intrapreneurs and for the development of an 'intraprise' in which these change masters can flourish.

Finally, in Part IV, I take you through the step-by-step process whereby you can develop yourself, as an intrepreneur, over the course of your working life.

In summary, I am undertaking the ambitious task, within this book, of helping you discover a new breed of manager. Whatever light I succeed in casting on the subject can only begin to illuminate the way. Progress in personal and business development will ultimately depend as much upon you, the reader, as upon me, the author. I hope between us we can both profit, and develop. Let me start then, with the underlying 'spectrum theory'.

Notes and references

1 An article in the popular American business magazine, *Business Week,* in June, 1980, appeared to start the ball rolling.
2 For example, see John Naisbitt's book *Megatrends,* published by Macdonald and Sons, 1984.
3 Macrae's article first appeared in *The Economist* in December 1976.
4 See Michael Maccoby's book *The Gamesman* (Torch Books, 1978) for an elaboration on this theme.

2 The spectrum theory

> In the past, people who were required to perform much physical labour, learned how to store up and release physical energy. Today we need to learn more about 'psychic energy', and how to release it.
>
> John Ingalls,
> *Human Energy and Organisation Development*

Intrapreneurs, like those described in this book, have striking personal qualities. Unlike the more impersonal 'manager', they are each very much their own person. To understand them therefore, we need a theory of personality that can uncover their underlying attitudes, motivation and behaviour.

I have chosen 'spectrum theory' for three reasons. First and foremost, it is a theory, at one and the same time, of personality, of management and of business. It enables us therefore to correlate one with the other. In other words, we can use a common language to describe people and business. Second, it is a practical model in that we can use it not only to describe intrapreneurs but also to develop them. Third, I have personally worked with spectrum theory, particularly with people developing businesses, over the past five years. The theory is therefore solidly grounded. In fact, its founder, Kevin Kingsland, has spent some twenty years testing the concepts with students of psychology and business. His experimental work, involving thousands of students, has been carried out in Britain and America, as well as in India and Australia.

What, then, is spectrum theory? Basically, it is a model of communication. We communicate in effect, across a 'spectrum'. People potentially give out and prospectively receive back, seven kinds of 'psychic energy'. John Ingalls, who spent many years applying his ideas in the American health services, has argued that – with the advance of automation – it is psychic, rather than physical energy, to which we must pay attention.

The seven kinds of personal energy – equivalent to the spectrum of colours in the rainbow – are full of latent potential as well as actual force. Each person is like seven floors of a building. On every floor a light of a different colour is shining. Imagine, in your mind's eye the seventh floor. Therein lies Inspiration. Picture another light one floor below – Intuition. Think of the fifth floor down – Authority. Spot the light on the next one – Willpower. Next comes Flexibility. Look for the bright light on the second one – Enthusiasm. Finally, switch on the light on the first, ground floor – Physical Energy.

We have all seven floors, all seven lights within us. But some are much more brightly lit than others. Through failing to communicate with certain types of people, we fail to communicate with certain parts of ourselves. One personality trait is likely to dominate. A couple of others will also be in evidence. And the rest will remain dimly lit, that is, until we acquire personal mastery.

Personality and communication

The key to personal mastery lies in communication. We become more 'colourful', and less stereotyped, when we open up the different sides of ourselves. A first step along the way is to open up to others.

Everything we do in life is essentially a manifestation of our self image. If we, as corporate people, identify entrepreneurship with small businesses, and management with large scale enterprise, then the die is cast. Similarly, if we consider imaginative people to be artists, and realistic people to be businessmen, then, if we are in business, we are left with no choice, except to be realistic!

Once, then, we have adopted a role, much of our behaviour becomes stereotyped. A vast cultural and organisational 'memory' provides scripts for every part. People who break out of the role are considered strange, or mavericks. Some organisations are open minded enough to encourage maverick behaviour, at least to an extent, but many are not.

So the individual identifies with some elements of his world, and not others. Although we all have access to a variety of types of behaviour, we tend to identify with some rather than others. Different personalities identify with different things: for example, colleagues, work, intellect, or family and friends. For effective management teamwork and development, it is necessary to know what the other person identifies with. For example, messages directed to the intellect may not touch a 'social' or 'physical' type. Communication will then fail, in the same way as 'management' and 'workers' often fail to make contact with one another.

If you know what a person identifies with, then his behaviour becomes more predictable. It is as if you had the precise co-ordinates of a person's whereabouts on the earth's surface. You could then go to that spot, as it were, and experience the same views as that person. In that way, for example, researcher and marketeer could understand one another's language. The key to such understanding lies not merely in appreciating one set of jargon or another, but in identifying with the other person's 'worldview'. If you stand your ground and the other person stands his, there is little chance of communications between you.

In fact, if you wish to be accepted by a person, and to influence him, you need to reinforce his sense of security. When a person feels secure he tends to communicate more freely. For some, 'security' lies in knowledge, for others it lies in friendship, and for others again, in material possessions. Recognising your own fears and security zones can give you an insight into other people's.

Communication requires work, whether the communication is with customers, employees, associates, or with yourself. If you are to make contact with different people, or with the different sides of yourself, it is essential to understand human personality. Recognising the personality spectrum, 'out there' leads to a developing sense of individuality, as you discover yourself mirrored in others. For example, if you are unable to identify with the 'marketing personality' in others, you will never discover it within yourself.

The personality spectrum

Each of us, as a whole, is a composite of seven parts. Each part/stereotype, brings with it prevailing tendencies. We can best discover each part of ourselves by recognising personal and intrapreneurial capacities in others as shown in Table 2.1.

Table 2.1
Spectrum of personality and intrapreneurship

Personality type	Intrapreneurial type	Key attributes
Imagination	Innovator	Originality, Inspiration, Love, Transformation
Intuition	New designer/ Enabler	Evolution, Development, Symbiosis, Connection
Authority	Leader	Direction, Responsibility, Structure, Control
Will	Entrepreneur	Achievement, Opportunity, Risk Taking, Power
Sociability	Animateur	Informality, Shared Values, Community, Culture
Energy	Adventurer	Movement, Work, Health, Activity
Flexibility	Charge agent	Adaptability, Expressiveness, Curiosity, Intelligence

Through the questionnaire on pages 16–19 you will be able to find out, in a rough and ready way, the kind of 'personality type' that you are. I say 'rough and ready' because there is more to each and every one of us than a personality, or intrapreneurial 'type'. In fact, the profile with which you will emerge, from the questionnaire, can only predict how you characteristically behave. It says little about your underlying, and often subconscious motives. Yet these form a significant part of your prospects for mastery.

In fact the seven masters, or intrapreneurs, whom we are about to meet, have each transcended their predominant trait. For example, while Conran is a Master of the Imagination and Harvey Jones is a Master of Organisation, there is more to each than imagination and organisation, respectively. They wear coats of many colours, even if one colour predominates. For to become an intrapreneur you require a powerful motive, and a reserve store of energy, as well as a particular basis for mastery. Whereas Conran's basis for mastery has been his creative imagination, his underlying motive has been to remove ugliness from the world, and his reserve store of energy provides him with flexibility and willpower. While Harvey Jones' powers of organisation have brought him to the top, his underlying motivation has been to involve people. At the same time, both physical stamina and an ability to cope with change have served him well.

But rather than continue in this sketchy vein I should now like to introduce you to the characters concerned. In each case I shall start with the individual, and then describe the relevant theory underpinning his or her particular role. This should enable you to place each of the seven 'archetypes' in a broader academic as well as business context.

Appendix – The spectral inventory

The 'spectral inventory', which is based on a model of communication and enterprise developed over fifteen years, is designed to 'profile' both your personality and leadership style. It is also used to profile the different activities in your ongoing business, or new business venture.

Put the statements in each of the following eight sets into rank order, from 7 (high) to 1 (low), to ensure that no two statements within a set have the same ranking, even if this leads to a 'forced' choice.

RANK

1 (a)   I am an active person who likes to keep
         physically on the go.
   (b)   I like to create something out of nothing,
         something which is completely original.
   (c)   I tend to let things flow, until something or
         someone meaningful emerges.
   (d)   I like to be the one in authority, so that
         I can keep things under control.
   (e)   I am willing to take a calculated risk, both
         with money and people.
   (f)   I respond to every situation differently.
   (g)   I enjoy being sociable.

2 (a)   I have lots of energy to do things.
   (b)   I am an inventive sort of a person, who
         always sees a new angle on things.
   (c)   I really enjoy seeing people develop to their
         full potential.
   (d)   I welcome the responsibility of organising
         people.
   (e)   I like to be in front.
   (f)   I enjoy mental stimulation.
   (g)   I value friendship above all things.

3 (a)   I love good food and wine.
   (b)   I like to dream, to build up a grand picture
         of how things ought to be.
   (c)   I rely on intuition rather than on logic.
   (d)   I follow procedures thoroughly.
   (e)   I like achieving tangible things.
   (f)   I reason things out in my own time.
   (g)   I feel good with lots of people.

4 (a)   I act quickly and don't look back
   (b)   I am a very imaginative person.
   (c)   I am often the one to create harmony
         between people.
   (d)   I am good at putting information and things
         into categories.
   (e)   I like to be totally committed.
   (f)   I have a logical approach.

 (g) I am usually the one who gives emotional support to people.

5 (a) I like physical exercise.
 (b) I can totally change a situation from one state into another.
 (c) I can see the pattern in events or relationships.
 (d) I like to be clear about my role.
 (e) I like to see a tangible return for my efforts, like money.
 (f) I like novelty in my work.
 (g) I find it easy to establish a warm atmosphere where people feel at home.

6 (a) Health comes first.
 (b) I am always looking for an opportunity to innovate.
 (c) I am an insightful person, who can understand people in depth.
 (d) I like creating order out of chaos.
 (e) I enjoy overcoming hurdles.
 (f) Living and learning is what it's all about.
 (g) I want to be recognised as a nice person.

7 (a) I like using my physical strength.
 (b) I want to be a source of inspiration to people around me.
 (c) I can identify the real meaning behind things.
 (d) I welcome a clearly defined chain of command.
 (e) I am very persistent in achieving my aims.
 (f) I am pretty flexible in my response to people and situations.
 (g) I spend lots of time with people I like.

8 (a) I do lots of sport, of one kind or another.
 (b) Creativity is my obsession.
 (c) I like dealing with opposites in people or ideas.
 (d) I am good at turning vague ideas into firm concepts.

RANK

(e)   I like uncertain situations, where there is
      room for manoeuvre.
(f)   I hate to be tied down.
(g)   I like to show people what I feel about them.

Now take the total rank score for all the (a) statements and plot it on the graph. Repeat for the (b) statements and so on.

Part II

Developing a vision – Terence Conran, innovator

3

The Habitat look has gathered an increasing number of converts as their eye becomes educated to appreciate fresh, simple and imaginative furnishing. Now, not only in furnishing, but also in toys and clothing, we are making good design accessible to everyone. Perhaps I'm helping to create a self-sufficient British industry, with design at the centre of it all.

Sir Terence Conran, Chairman, Habitat-Mothercare

'I was born into a typical middle class family, where my father just managed to make ends meet. He spent more money sending us to good schools than on anything else. But fortunately for my sister and I, our schools were very different from the average. There was a very strong creative bias and I had an inspired man called Don Potter to teach me craft subjects. With him I worked in metal, wood and clay.

That gave me a great desire to make artefacts. I set myself up with a workshop at home, and built my own pottery kiln. I also did a lot of welding. But to make the activity viable, I had to sell my wares. I found some unwilling relations, and can also remember making things for a local toy shop. I was 13 at the time, and it was during the war years.

One memory that stands out, is of a typical English pottery in Farnham. They made terra cotta flower and chimney pots.

It was a completely self contained unit. They dug the clay themselves, made the pots, and then sold them on the spot, from a builders merchant's yard. They even made use of the local farmer's wasted pea sticks for firing the kiln. I used to cycle 17 miles there and 17 miles back to be part of this compact and fascinating business. I remember working at a foot-pedal wheel, making little flower pots. A penny for five. Funnily enough I enjoyed doing one, repetitively, after another.

I loved the whole circular process, from digging at one end to selling at the other. It was a wonderful example of self sufficiency.

I carried on at school, and completed my higher certificate in organic chemistry, engineering and art. I didn't have a clue, at that stage, what to do with my life. A friend maintained that organic chemistry and drawing were linked. I was also very interested in things botanical, which involved all kinds of shapes and forms. So it was suggested that I do textile design. I was apparently good at recognising, understanding, and detailing relationships in artefacts, in plants, and in chemistry. So I took a course at the Central School of Arts and Crafts in London, in textile design.

I became very interested, immediately, in the process of screen printing. I found the historical aspect fascinating. I used to go off to the Victoria and Albert Museum. I also worked in the evenings for one of my tutors. He used to produce Matisse panels. Each would fetch a million dollars, today, but those times were still very austere. To find cloth we had to go down to Petticoat Lane and search around for it.

After about eighteen months at Central School I began to get itchy feet. I had become friendly with the sculptor, Eduardo Palozzi. We shared a workshop in Bethnal Green. He taught me form and I taught him practical skills. At that stage I was really beginning to get interested in making furniture for myself. There was nothing on the market that I liked. So I started making things for myself and for friends. I had a particular style.

Then I was offered a job by a design centre in Grosvenor Street. I was in charge of the library, the exhibition area and the studio. I also got involved in producing a quarterly magazine. It was 1949. Britain was just starting to pull itself together after the war. The architect who brought me into the design centre decided to go off on his own, and took me with him. We did a lot of work for the Homes and Gardens section, in the Festival Exhibition that year. I even did the interior design for a flying boat. I wish I had kept a picture of it.

There was terrific enthusiasm at the exhibition. The designers thought that the new world had come. But the energy began to dry up, as the exhibition wore on. Industry failed to seize the opportunity. The UK was still in the economic doldrums. So we got no more work. I lost my £8 a week, and got a job doing window display at Simpsons. At the same time I continued to make furniture and to do textile designs. I found a few customers for textile designs like Myers beds and Edinburgh Weavers.

Simpsons said to me, "We don't sell many shoes in August, so why don't you exhibit your furniture in the shoe department". I got a few orders and moved my workshop from Bethnal Green to Sloane Square. I even employed somebody. My career in industry had begun!

I had to start thinking more seriously, then, about selling. I was terribly inept on the business side. But I didn't mind doing it. Things were always hand to mouth. I used to try and deliver furniture by underground. There had to be more to life than this! So I started to consider, in greater depth, design philosophy, and its importance to industry and society. I was convinced that design added to the quality of life. And everything made is designed. *I felt very deeply that well designed artefacts should be made available to people at a mass level. So all through my early career I was addressing the question, how am I going to get out of this narrow backwater, and touch the real world?*

I seemed to spend my entire life in basements. I progressed, at this stage, from a basement workshop in Sloane Square to one in Notting Hill Gate, immediately beneath the intense noise of Ballet Rambert's dancing feet. Soon after that I moved on to a Piccadilly arcade, underneath a flower shop. I employed someone to sell my furniture and produced my first brochure. Then I moved in to cheap and derelict premises in Chelsea, a funny narrow building. It became my first factory. Believe it or not Sir Clive Sinclair has now bought it, to convert into a house.

Actually, that's the way we accumulated a little capital, in those days. We renovated the buildings we moved into, and then sold them off. Nevertheless, I was always desperately short of money. And I desperately wanted to make some, to buy machinery. A psychiatrist friend of mine at the time was also broke. Together we hit on the idea of a café-cum-soup kitchen, with different soups, French bread and the second Expresso making machine in the country. Soon we had created a chain of four, and when I eventually sold my share to him, I made a bit of money. We had sensed a need, and exploited it.

In the mid fifties, most of the furniture we were making was specified by architects for offices, hotels and hospitals. It was a boom time for that sort of building. There was very little stylish furniture around. I started up a textiles conversion business, buying cloth, or having it woven, and re-selling it. Soon after that we got involved with shopfitting, and with selling exhibition stands. In fact, we designed the early shops for Mary Quant.

Then we made a quantum leap, moving from two inefficient factories in London to Thetford in Norfolk. In the fifties, the GLC would build a factory for you outside of London, and then rent it. It was a fascinating time, having to convince 80 people to move to the Norfolk countryside. We took them and their families on bus trips to Norfolk. I enjoyed the whole business of making the move, and thinking about people's lives in that way.

When we got to the new factory it was a wonderful, clean and efficient space. It was difficult to adjust though, from workshop to factory techniques. I hadn't realised how much we could produce with all the new plant we had. So we decided, for the first time, to make a range of domestic furniture. It was 1962. We took a space at the Furniture Exhibition at Earls Court. Our furniture had a somewhat similar look to that in a Habitat store today.

We sold the furniture to about 80 different retailers around the country. Then we went off to see how it looked. We were appalled. The quality of display, of presentation, was terribly poor. But what could we do? A company like 'G' Plan did their own display within somebody else's store. That cost money we couldn't afford. *So we tried to open a prototype shop ourselves embodying various principles. Above all, it had to look busy. Most furniture shops are great stagnant pools filled with brown lumps of scum! A shop needs customers in it to keep staff on their toes.*

We developed our prototype, with 50 per cent furniture and 50 per cent other household goods, like kitchen utensils, lighting and floor coverings. We also knew that our customers would be young, so we incorporated a toy department. The shop opened with lots of publicity, though we'd had no experience in retailing. We made every mistake under the sun! But we had enough energy and life to ride over the problems. At the time, the new look clothes shops were just opening. There were lots of Italian restaurants. There was the beginning of a feeling of change, and our shop fitted perfectly into this. Of course the other retailers insisted that it was one thing for us to succeed in London, but we wouldn't have a hope in Manchester.

Unlike those retailers, we sensed the signs of the times; we had insight into our market potential. There was the odd shop like us in Scandinavia, but nothing more. Seven years ago I discovered that there were 85 Habitats in America, all trying to copy us. They were ten years behind.

One important thing that we did was to fill our shop with stock. In other furniture stores 'we'll order it for you', was the approach. But we used the supermarket approach of making the goods available on the shelves. The stocky, warehouse feel was very attractive to the customers. We provided an exciting environment for them.

After that early period of getting to know the ropes, and experiencing the frustrations of learning from our own mistakes, *we began to realise we enjoyed retailing, and making ourselves visible on the High Street. We believed it would work in Manchester. So the idea of a retail chain came to us. That meant we would really have to teach ourselves retailing, including distribution, stock control, and so forth.*

We also formed the very positive opinion that the future, for retailing, lay in creating something unique, something different from other people's shops. Habitat things were designed by us, not by manufacturer 'X'. By capturing a unique market niche, moreover, we would avoid being involved in constant price battles.

That was our initial approach. In order to uphold it, we had to expand fast in order to give the manufacturers large enough throughput to make things economical. Through the 1960s we progressed smoothly with just one major hiccup. We merged with Rymans, who had been good customers of ours in contract furnishing. The opportunities in office furnishing were very good at the time. So most of our energy was put into the Rymans side, and poor Habitat became the Cinderella. Whereas that may have been best for the company as a whole, my real interest was in Habitat. So I agreed, with the Rymans people, to buy Habitat out, leaving behind our design consultancy and manufacturing interests. The design group, which has since become Fitch and Co., is now a highly successful one.

Around that time I did make a lot of money. Burton bought up Rymans at a very good price, and I had retained a 20 per cent interest. That gave me real capital to expand Habitat, from its 1971 turnover of two and a half million pounds. We went at it singlemindedly. If London and Manchester, why not Paris or New York? If America, why not Japan? We came to believe that the Western World was our market. If you have an original retailing concept it can span frontiers.

With a view to setting up in America, we started looking for finance. It was difficult to persuade the UK banks that we were something other than a trendy shop like a jeans boutique. So we ended up with a Dutch bank. I got very close to Hugo Harbosh, one of its directors and invited him to become a non-executive director of Habitat. It was he who seeded the idea that we should be applying our design and retailing philosophy to companies other than ourselves. It was purely coincidental that Mothercare, who had always been generous to us with their computer facilities, and whom we greatly admired, were reviewing their future direction at the time.

Selim Zhilka had built up a fine business which had many parallels with Habitat. Both companies were specialist retailers who did a high percentage of their business through mail order catalogues, and both addressed themselves to the same target customer. But Mothercare had slipped downmarket in recent years. Selim Zhilka, an extremely astute man, knew, when his profits began to fall, that it was because his merchandise had become lacklustre. He recognised the cure in the design-led Habitat concept. So I took over his business, and the alliance has proved a great success. Both companies have learnt a lot from one another. We now have the best retail systems in the world, along with our unique design philosophy.

I then realised that there must be many other similar opportunities. We have taken over Richard Shops and Heals, and are busy putting our design ability into them. A major practical attraction in both cases in fact, was an extremely advantageous property deal. But, whereas with Richard Shops just about everything else with it was wrong, Heals did have a reputation for well-designed, high quality merchandise. I also have an architecturally based consultancy company, Conran–Roche, which is periodically involved in property development. Finally, I recently formed an alliance with Paul Hamlyn at Octopus publishing. This joint venture will provide an opportunity to link the Habitat design-based approach to living, with Octopus' expertise in publishing and marketing.

One of the things I'm proudest of is my relationship with the people in our organisation. After reading about the American system of share ownership, we decided to set up something similar in this country. Together with a firm of consultants in this field we managed to formulate an idea of what we'd like to achieve, based on the profitability of the company. Given an upper limit, employees were eligible to share in the profits of their part of the business. I made over 25 per cent of my shareholding to this Employee Share Scheme Fund. We were the first company to do this sort of thing in Britain, and we had enormous difficulties with the Inland Revenue. But the whole idea was to make our company a better one, by making people feel it is theirs. The effect on morale has been pretty good. In fact, in the last ten years, none of our senior management has left. The company is expanding and they have a real interest in it.

We're on the edge now, of getting to my eventual ambition. The strength of the original Habitat design-based formula has been in selling furniture in a colourful ambiance partially created by the non-furniture merchandise. We have sold products which all measure up to a good standard of design, and appear to have been selected with 'one pair of eyes'. We have invested in a large design team, to ensure exclusivity, well designed merchandise and strong graphic style. Moreover, we have never been satisfied with existing standards. Now, we are really developing and diversifying our retail operations, well beyond furniture, and should soon be touching all socio-economic groupings.

Two things are happening in the marketplace. Retailers are coming to understand that they can exercise their power to create products unique to them. Also, there is a new breed of buyer in the retail world who is a creative person rather than a number cruncher. So the buyers are able to work alongside designers and manufacturers to create innovative merchandise. Secondly, more and more people are realising how bad so many shops are. At the same time a lot of electronic developments are giving the manufacturer the lead time they need. Shops have got to become less like a visit to the dentist, and more pleasant and exciting.

What I enjoy most now is the feeling that we can make any product we require, thanks to our designers' abilities. Richard Shops for example, is a huge turnaround project, creating new products, new management, new systems. The task is the same for Heals. The great thing is to have matters under your control, not to be the hostage of other people's fortunes. These are our products. This is our style. We will take responsibility for the manufacturing. Hence we have the courage of our convictions. We've created and stand by our own case in the high streets. Everything is under our control.

People have probably not yet recognised the effect that a successful, imaginative retailer can have on the economy. We have caused manufacturers to improve their standards, and UK manufacturers cannot compete internationally on price alone. If you couple design talent with efficient and flexible manufacturing capability, you have a formula for success.

So, the way I see it, manufacturing is accepting this change in the style of retailing very constructively. When we went to Mothercare's exclusive suppliers, Courtaulds for example, the speed with which they welcomed our change in approach to design was remarkable. I see ourselves collaborating more and more with manufacturers to produce better designed products.

Design, essentially, is a matter of function, taste and style. It involves a feeling for mood. A good designer can express a mood before the population has realised what is happening to it. Through observing what people are doing, feeling and thinking, he sensitively captures something in the air and reveals it into, say, clothes or furnishing. The result excites people's imagination. That's something the Japanese are particularly good at. They do so much looking before they decide on anything. I spoke to a Japanese the other day who had gone to eight universities and taken two million pictures of people and what they were wearing. The Japanese are not great style innovators, but they understand a feeling.

We on the other hand, have created a style. Through Habitat, well designed furniture and furnishings are now accessible to people of modest means, whereas twenty years ago they were the prerogative of the well off. As Habitat's success has demonstrated, this availability has changed the way people furnish their homes. The Habitat look has gathered an increasing number of converts as their eye becomes educated to appreciate fresh, simple and imaginative furnishing. Now, not only in furnishing, but also in toys and clothing, we are making good design accessible to everyone. Perhaps I'm helping to create a self-sufficient British industry, with design at the centre of it all.'

****
Developing a vision
****

– introducing creativity and **imagination**

the innovator has the ability to imagine or envision the future

– **bettering** humanity

the highest use of money is for the betterment of life

– **transforming** dreams into reality

the true innovator lives in both the worlds of imagination and concrete reality

– innovation as a **passion**

creativity and innovation is an immensely personal process

– acquiring **mastery**

the innovator is master of himself and his circumstances

– going back to **origins**

the genuine innovator uncovers and transforms the roots of technology and society

imagine – how do you envisage the future?

- How do you envisage the future?
- What innovation have you pictured in your mind?
- What little corner of the infinite has been revealed to you?

betterment – how do you impart values?

- How are you bettering life?
- What is your vision of service?
- What, in the language of uplift and idealism is distinctive about your enterprise?

transform – what dream are you turning into a reality?

- What are you adding to the totality of things?
- How are you transforming reality?
- How are you fitting all the pieces together into a new order?

passion – what do you love?

- What do you love about your business?
- What makes you experience sheer ecstasy?
- What intense encounters do you engage in?

mastery – how have you mastered yourself and your business?

- What enduring ambition are you fulfilling?
- How do you master time, in all its dimensions?
- How are you becoming a master of your own life?

originality – what are your origins?

- What historic sense, and sensibility, lie within you?
- What lies at the root of your company's being?
- How have those roots been imaginatively woven into a story of the business?

****

Introducing creativity and IMAGINATION

Terence Conran was, and is, an innovator. As such, he has the ability to imagine, or envision the future. In the process he creates a product or a service. He therefore possesses:

- an ability to visualise things or events
- an ability to foresee the future
- a means of escape from everyday reality
- the power to deal with things or situations not physically present
- the ability to invent, to produce works of art, or to create a new order of things

Innovation is an intensely personal, as well as being a dramatic, and gripping activity. It needs to be gripping in order to sustain effort, as in Conran's case, for over thirty years. A group of American sociologists, in an extremely good, 1964 study of innovators and entrepreneurs, put it this way:

> Despite all initial misgivings, the creator eventually works as though he expected to realise his dream. He is intent. His mind is not inhibited into dumb neutrality by any fear of making the wrong decisions. In the secrecy of his heart, he believes that what he is attempting may add to the totality of things. And, as he progresses, it becomes more and more evident to him that he is on the right road, his timidity is thrown to the winds. He presides for the moment like a God over the little corner of this infinite which has revealed itself to him, and which in just this manner has revealed itself to none before him.[1]

BETTERING Humanity

For the innovator, it is not money that is the ultimate arbiter of his conduct. It is his idea. For Conran the idea of making simple, tasteful products accessible to all has been his obsession. Conran has more than a little in common with Henry Ford.

Ford was a man similarly obsessed. Yet, interestingly

enough, for two hundred years, we have been much more interested in following the words and principles of Adam Smith, rather than those of Henry Ford. And the one created a textbook and the other an automobile industry. Strange it is, but true. I would venture to guess that management, even at Ford, are more familiar with laissez faire economics than with the writings and philosophies of their founding father.

My own memory of Ford, when I can dismiss from my mind his personal idiosyncracies and miserable prejudices, is that of the man of true vision, the great innovator, who stood up on the platform and proclaimed:

> As far as individual personal advantage is concerned, vast accumulations of money mean nothing. But if one has visions of service, if one has vast plans which no ordinary resources could possibly realize, if one has a life ambition to make the industrial desert bloom like the rose, and the work-day-life suddenly blossom into fresh and enthusiastic human motives of higher character and efficiency than one sees in large sums of money, then one sees what the farmer envisions in his seed corn – the beginning of new and richer harvests whose benefits can no more be selfishly confined than the sun's rays.[2]

Conran's analogous life ambition is to make the retail desert bloom!

TRANSFORMING dreams into reality

An innovator, like Terence Conran, is different from an entrepreneur, like Richard Branson or Tiny Rowlands. For the entrepreneur, the building blocks for his creation already exist – that is the people, the finance, the facilities, and the product or service. What is new is the way they are put together. But, for the innovator, some, if not all the components will be mere ideas. These will have to be turned into concrete reality, with all the difficulties and hazards which that involves, before their incorporation in the new arrangement can ever begin. So the original furniture that Terence Conran designed had to be displayed in newly created retail setting before they could become accessible.

In converting his idea into concrete reality, the innovator links two human worlds, two kinds of human activity; it might even be said, two kinds of people. The first group finds the world of thought and imagination real and satisfying, and the second demand of something new that it can be touched and measured, before it can be taken seriously. Conran lives in both of these worlds, at one and the same time. He forms the bridge between art and design, on the one hand, and operations and marketing on the other.

Innovation as a PASSION

Twenty years after Conran established the first Habitat, an American journalist by the name of Tracy Kidder published the contemporary best seller, *The Soul of the New Machine*. The book was based on the American computer company, Data General. Its hero is a computer programmer 'extraordinaire' by the name of West. Mr West was the head of a project to produce a new computer, with expanded memory capacity, in record time:

> For some time, during the debugging of the first Eclipse [new model of computer], West was ill every morning before work – a prephological form of morning sickness, perhaps. But when the job was done he went to the factory floor and saw a long file of brand new Eclipses come gliding down a conveyor belt. Some great delight, which he could describe as almost a chemical change came over him.

West is an innovator, who not only produces an end product but also experiences 'morning sickness'. The analogy with human birth and procreation is absolutely fitting. Creativity and innovation is an immensely personal process:

> Writing microcode (machine translation language) is like nothing else in my life. For days there's nothing coming out. The empty yellow pad sets there in front of me, reminding me of my inadequacy. Finally it starts to come. I feel good. That feeds it, and finally I get into a state where I'm a microcode writing machine. It's like being in Adventure. Adventure is a completely bogus world, but when you're there, you're there.[3]

West, in the book and probably in reality, had two great loves, music and computers. Perhaps he considered himself a 'balladeer of computers', in the same way as Conran has become a 'designer of retailing'.

Acquiring MASTERY

As 'balladeer of computers', West had become joyful master of his own destiny. Similarly, the successful enterprise will be one that is balanced between its short-term needs and long-term requirements. The 'intrapreneur' at the helm will have developed a mastery, over himself and his situation, enabling him to harness inner motivation and outer momentum.

Alistair Mant, a management educator and longstanding critic of bureaucratic management, contrasts 'bi-podal' and 'tri-podal' 'leadership'. Whereas the first kind, which, he says, might be called 'transactional', is survival oriented, the second is 'transformational' and inspired by some imagined state of corporate being. Above all, the tri-podal manager has the ability to stand back and view things with perspective. He is therefore able to become master of himself and his circumstances, whereas his bi-podal counterpart can easily become the victim of both.

Elliot Jacques, a longtime student of leadership and organisation in Great Britain links the 'touch of greatness' with the 'time span of discretion', that an individual can sustain. The very best people, he says, can 'envision very long periods of time', and handle the multiple of resulting abstractions, from the front line through to the Chairman's desk. They can become, therefore, total masters of the unfolding situation. Conran started Habitat in 1964, and it is only now that he can see his original dream, of a design-led retailing revolution, coming true.

Going back to ORIGINS

So the innovative idea emerges from a long way back in history. Innovators retrace steps to the roots of a particular art or science. Conran was inspired by the Bauhaus School that created industrial design in 1919. For many of his furniture ranges, he drew on classical designs that date back hundreds of years. Each range tells its own story. With people, as with products:

> When we are free to create or discover and live our own individual myths, when we begin to write and enact our own story, then we will have begun to live creatively.[4]

Only when original roots are discovered and extended, can healthy branches be grown. The genuine innovator, therefore, uncovers and transforms the roots of both the technology and the society, with which he is involved. That is true originality. Terence Conran has drawn on classical furniture designs in order to create his unique and contemporary 'lifestyle' image. All truly creative people have stood on the shoulders of giants.

Conclusion

An innovator like Conran transforms something ethereal into a physical entity, that is needed by society at large. In the process he draws upon the origins of an art or science, and taps the hidden depths of a latent need. He becomes master of his circumstances and engages with passion in fashion or automobiles, furniture or artifical intelligence. He seeks to improve the society in which he is living, through his idea, and can hold in his imagination a picture of what he intends to create. He is seldom good at managing, in conventional terms, because that requires too much pre-established order. He is not an entrepreneur, in the normal sense, because making money is merely a means to an end. Financial reward is much less important to him than the realisation of an idea, the creation of an image.

Unlike the pure scientist or artist, however, he is intent on meeting a powerful, often subconscious, customer need. Terence Conran has not been in the business of transforming people's homes just for art's sake. He has both cultivated and satisfied the need for tasteful products – originally in furnishing, and furniture accessories, and now in books, toys and – most especially – clothing. Conran was and is a creative intrapreneur, a genuine visionary. He has combined thought, emotion and action over time and over space – from childhood to adulthood, and from Iceland to Japan.

References

1   Collins, O., Moore, D., and Unwalla, D., *Enterprising Man,* Michigan University, 1964.
2   Ford, Henry, *My Life and Years,* Crowell, New York, 1922.
3   Kidder, Tracy, *The Soul of the New Machine,* Penguin Books, Harmondsworth, 1982.
4   Kopp, Sheldon, *If you meet Buddha on the road – kill him!,* Sheldon Press, London, 1974.

Harnessing potential – Mary Quant, 'new designer'

4

Style and fashion anticipates and forecasts, expressing a mood and a state of mind. Fashion permanently changes. It is affected by what takes. Once it has taken it is no longer interesting. There is an inevitable progression.

Mary Quant, Founder, Mary Quant Ltd.

Alexander

The context. England and London after the war. You wouldn't have thought the war had ended in 1945.

Mary and I met each other at art school. School was disappointing. Life was drab, squalid and depressed. Teenagers fighting in the war had missed their youth. After the war, we still suffered, particularly visually. We were in a vacuum.

We were an unusual generation. Something had to be done. We saw ourselves as totally different from our parents. In fact we viewed ourselves as revolutionary. Terence Conran, John Osborne, David Bailey – a few of us decided we had to take matters into our own hands. We had no business education, but it didn't matter.

Archie MacNair, our partner and now our Chairman, who had trained as a lawyer, started by opening the first coffee bar in London. I had inherited £5000. We plunged in, wanting to liberate ourselves from the puritanical generation that preceded us. We wanted to democratise things – food, design, music. His coffee bar became a social centre in Chelsea. We used to sit up and talk all night. *Archie had already spotted a cultural abyss. There was nowhere for people to go, and meet. Mary saw that the clothes were all wrong too.* She had this passion about clothes. So we opened a dress shop in 1955, Bazaar, in the King's Road. We didn't have the faintest idea about invoices or anything like that. But the clothes were cheap, uncompromising, and revolutionary. People had never seen anything like it. Skimpy. Childish. They made young women look like naughty children! Bright colours. Show off. The effect was electric.

It was more successful than anything we might have expected. Eccentric clothes for eccentric people. It turned out we were typical of our generation. But, within the year, we recognised that this was an arrogant view. *We had, in fact, spotted a 'uniform' that everyone wanted all over the world.*

People didn't have much money at the time, so they couldn't afford to go to fancy restaurants. So young people ended up eating fish and chips or going to the pubs, which were unattractive. *Now, for the first time, the young grasped the opportunity, to get together, and to start businesses for their peers.* We made every mistake, businesswise, in the book of course. *Soon we went from one coffee bar to two and three. They became centres for architects, painters, sculptors, tarts and con men!* But, after a while we wanted to expand, and therefore we sold the restaurant to raise equity, in order to finance more shops.

It seems, in retrospect, pure luck that it all turned out right. Our first shop had proved a terrifying success. People came from all over Europe. So we opened two more. A second Bazaar in Knightsbridge, designed by Terence Conran, opened in 1957 and a third in Bond Street, in 1967. Our inefficiency created headaches for poor Archie later on.

Our next step was to expand into all sorts of different

product areas, to persuade people to make their products in other ways. Archie promulgated that approach. And he put together the whole licensing idea — the basis for the business now.

Mary

We started terribly small. I bought fabric from Harrods, employed two or three machinists, and made items up. We opened a workroom. I went along to knitwear manufacturers and persuaded one or two to make their cardigans a foot longer, turning them into knitted dresses or coats. Of course, most of them thought I was mad. The clothes and dresses just slid over, creating a body shape.

I didn't like stiffness or artificiality. I didn't want to grow up. I wanted people to wear flatter shoes and to move, run, dance. The image first came to me when I was eight. A tap dancer with a bullet haircut, wearing black tights, black shirt, black patent leather shoes, and white socks. This black and white image branded my mind. That was it. It stuck with me for ever.

There have been variations on the black and white theme, bringing in the element of surprise, and putting the spotlight on legs. But it has remained the background to the changing colours up front. Vidal Sassoon did the hair that went with the clothes in the mid sixties. In the meantime, I had been asked by the American chain store, J.C. Penney, to design fashions for their stores throughout America. It all happened when we took a trip over to America, penniless. I had three telephone numbers. Important ones, including Life Magazine. Eventually I plucked up the courage and Life came to see us. They went crazy about our designs and attracted the attention of all sorts of companies, including J.C. Penney. I went onto design exclusive dresses for several American manufacturers and Butterick, in the United States, published my paper patterns for home dressmakers. We also launched sportswear for worldwide distribution, and a company called Alligator, in this country, started to make rainwear to my design.

Alexander

At that point the cosmetic companies got interested. Why had we left the face out? A small English company, run by an Anglophile American, approached us. For eighteen months we worked like hell, starting from scratch. It was frightening. It terrified me, but we had marvellous people to help us. In 1966 Mary Quant cosmetics was born.

Mary

I wanted the lines to be black, white and silver. The colour was the product. It could be photographed. Precise. The nail varnish related to the clothes. Camel and white, silver, yellow and red. And then there were the lipsticks. We used our friends as models. They were top models in their own right, and they used colour like an impressionist painter, rather than like a lacquer. By using a shading effect, they created an illusion of in and out on their faces. Taking their faces as a flat canvas . . .

Vidal Sassoon, as I have already indicated, *was creating a sophisticated simplicity. He cut hair as you would cut a fabric. So, together, we covered head to toe. Tunics. Tights. Dresses.* Back to that tap dancer. *Flat shoes. Hair. Fashion and Furniture. It all fitted together.*

Photography was very important. The look was photographic. The whole thing interlocked. The look was a model look. The clothes were pinned flat to the shop wall. It brought in people every week. Every week they were in for a surprise.

The clothes were very masculine. We used men's shirts in new ways, to project the femaleness of a woman.

Alexander

It was witty too. But, apart from luck, what made everything happen was a positively evangelical determination expressed in terms of fun, design and wit. Ultimately, we took ourselves terribly seriously. We spanned the whole style of life.

The mini skirt made Mary a world celebrity. In 1964 the Beatles went to New York, and London became the cultural capital of the world. Their girl friends were our models. Lennon bought his cap from us. The whole thing snowballed.

But *we never really got involved with manufacturing ourselves.* We realised we would never cope. So *we went the licensing route. In 1963 we entered into our first major agreement, with Nylon Hosiery. We still work together 21 years later. In 1968 we got together with Dupont and in 1970 with ICI, to promote Mary's co-ordinated range of household furnishings and domestic textiles.* By this stage we had come to realise that we could do the same thing for the home as we had done for the person.

The relationship between ourselves and our thirty licensees is like that between an advertising agent and a client. Our rewards are directly related to our sales. So we only select manufacturers who have a good distribution facility, and can provide profitable business for us.

The licensing also enables Mary to go worldwide, facilitating on the spot sales in the various countries concerned. But we don't grasp at just any opportunity. We probably get three approaches a week, and turn down most.

In 1972 we launched Mary's bedwear and curtains, with Carrington Viyella, and we also got involved in designing 'Daisy Doll' clothes and accessories. In 1974, ICI linked up with us to promote a Crimplene range. In 1977, Mary designed sunglasses for Polaroid, and in 1978 linked up with a Scottish carpet manufacturer to design patterned Axminster carpets. By 1982 Mary Quant shoes were launched, and, most recently, we have gone into stationery, with W.H. Smith.

Mary

Fashion permanently changes. It is affected by what takes. Once it has taken it is no longer interesting. There is an inevitable progression. Once something is successful it becomes hackneyed. There is a swing, a reaction. So you go back and forward between the tailored or the modern, the romantic or the bold and strong. Sometimes they proceed in parallel, or even get mixed together. Anything fresh, any new variation, looks interesting.

Style and fashion anticipates and forecasts, expressing a mood and a state of mind. In the sixties, for example, you had a childlike exuberance, expressing both economic and sexual emancipation. Then it swung back to nostalgia. You also got the celebration of women's new roles. As they became involved in tough jobs, so they began wearing men's clothes. In a way that made them look even more feminine. Both attraction and expression came together to give the clothes even more power. At the same time, the clothes were worn big, to give the impression of physical frailty. So quite a lot was being expressed all at once.

Up till 1969 I had really concentrated on fashion. It was the time of woman's emancipation. But the sixties were coming to an end, and people were turning broody and having babies. They were converting their crash pads into homes. So I turned my mind to putting together a home from top to toe. Duvets had started coming in. I gave them the stark modern look. You could put one cover in the washing machine and, with the other, change the entire mood of your bedroom.

Alexander

There was a colour explosion in the home. You could do the same for bedding as for clothes. Then came carpets. New patterns. New ideas.

Mary

My eye just keeps finding things in new combinations. Sometimes I see things that look wrong together. Anything. Two straps may be tied in a certain way. A fabric may be woven in a particular style. In the back of my mind I can see the textures and the colours. It's not restlesssness as much as renewal. Most of us are lazy. We stop looking and appreciating. Things tend to deteriorate. Then, if arranged in a particular way, we look again. Every room, for example, has its special atmosphere and its special needs but must be part of a whole. So I designed a collection of wallpapers to give people the freedom to create a unique interior by taking a selection of designs through various colour-ways. I like a mixture of scale and pattern. I love to juxtapose the bold with the delicate, old with new, the tailored with the romantic, each complementing each other.

Alexander

In 1971 we started to bring our cosmetics over to Japan. We slowly built that up. Whereas in other countries, primarily in the UK and USA, we have gone the licensing way, *Japan has done so well because it is a joint venture.*

Mary

So, over the last fourteen years, we have been enabling Japanese women to express themselves in new ways. As you can see, I'm still concerned with the democratising of fashion, but with a different emphasis. There are many more variables. For example, here is a shoe, made of leather, but deliberately made to look like rubber. Or you could do it the other way around. PVC could be made to look more appealing. The amusements of the mind and I. Making something interesting, different. If the shapes of clothes aren't changing that much, then the detail becomes more important.

What I'm doing now is what I dreamt about as a child. I'm fulfilling my dream. And what I find particularly exciting is working with a team. That's a development for me, a transition I had to make.

As for the future, I hope it will develop the way it's going. I can't say exactly where. It's very difficult, for example, to specify product areas. They change all the time. What is a leotard? In the dictionary it's a body stocking. Then it becomes a vest, and then shorts or something. Dance. Sports. Underwear. Overwear. All my designs relate to each other in endless variation.

It's the way I think, making jumps, moving diagonally, circling or curving. It's a female approach, although I notice a lot of successful men have it. That's the way our company works, allowing people to cross over diagonally, from one position to another, when the opportunity arises. That kind of diagonal route is providing more potential for women to develop their roles in organisations.

Of course, I am very much part of my time. I'm fairly typical in having an exciting job, and a house, and a marriage, and a garden, as women do now. It's a balancing trick.

Alexander

You could draw an analogy between what Mary was, in this country in 1960, and what she is in Japan now. A Joan of Arc figure. Sophisticated simplicity. Mary has been adopted by our Japanese company. *We're now very familiar with the scene over there. The thing is, we haven't gone in on top of them. We deliberately set up a real partnership.* We try to listen and understand. In fact, practically everyone we work with, we like as people. There is a great deal of thought and sympathy, of built in trust and mutual understanding between ourselves and our 'partners'. It was a stroke of luck. The people we work with are straight as a die. Nakayana, the boss, is an Anglophile. *There's real empathy between* us, as there is between *all of us here, working together.* There are just twenty of us in the building, and *we're a very close-knit group.* Our cleaner joined when she was 60 and she is now 85. She still wears a pair of Mary's high fashion boots!

Mary

What I do want to do is to open my own shops again, to gain direct access to the public.

Alexander

Licensing is a low-risk activity. But it makes you extremely vulnerable. We have to get closer to the ultimate retailer. On the licensing side, though, we have an administrative director who knows more than most lawyers about licensing. Our agreements are amongst the tightest around. We spend thousands protecting our trademarks in all countries. They tend to change according to whom you are dealing with. You could be involved, with a particular licensee, in twenty five different designs, each having six colour variations. In the more complex situations, the royalty is commensurately higher. Our total licensing turnover is about £800 000, on a retail value of £50 million, and our Japanese business is now running into seven figures.

Mary

Design can be applied to anything. We're now looking at computers. They're bound to become a fashion item. But, as yet, they haven't become female. Little girls want to make things. Boys like to play with them.

Alexander

We're feeling our way into computer programmes. We have a son of twelve. The very young are all into computers, especially the boys.

Mary

Young people are making their own things again. There is a parallel between our time, in the fifties, and the present day. There's a similar mood in Japan. A friendly energy. Now videos of pop music, are becoming fashion films. Design leads rather than follows. It has to be innovative. Design always anticipates.

****
Harnessing potential
****

– **harmonising** yin (feminine) with yang (masculine)

combining sensitive awareness with penetrating analysis

– recognising **intuitive** capacities

incorporating judgement, insight and foresight

– **developing** people and organisation

displaying empathy, establishing linkages, and harnessing potential

– **symbiosis** through joint ventures

in which companies feed off one another for mutual benefit

– recognising market **coincidence** and potential

uncovering patterns of demand and turning the wheels of fortune

– developing communication **networks**

through combining people and sources of information

harmony – can you recognise true harmony when you see it?
– Do you emphasise reciprocal influences?
– Are you able mutually to benefit individual and organisation?
– Do you have a talent for invoking consensus?

intuition – have you a feel for the whole order of things?
– Can you tolerate ambiguity?
– Are you willing to be surprised?
– Do you have a good feeling for market potential?

development – can you stimulate potential in people and business?
– Do you help individuals grow and become creative?
– Do you allow patterns of activity, and demand, their natural flow of development?
– Can you open up fresh pathways of thought and action?

symbiosis – do you enable people to feed off one another?
– Can you unite the complementary strengths of two individuals or companies?
– Are you able to devise successful ways of 'piggy-backing', for both parties concerned?
– Do you engage in long-term partnerships with customers, suppliers and others?

coincidence – how do you attract good luck?
– Do you welcome chance intrusions?
– Can you easily connect like with unlike?
– Are you fascinated by coincidence?

networks – are you a link-man between people and between products?
– Are you moored by many lines of connection?
– Can you build alliances?
– Are you able to construct networks of mutual support and enrichment?

****

Total innovators like Terence Conran or Henry Ford are rare birds indeed. They are in fact much rarer even than business leaders, like John Harvey Jones. Yet, falling somewhere in between the innovator and the business leader is a newly emerging breed of 'intrapreneur'. I call him or her a 'new designer', and sincerely believe their ranks will swell in the immediate future. Mary Quant is a particularly well known case in point. The 'new designer' is concerned as much with organisation design as with product, interior or systems design. She therefore 'enables' development of each.

Webster's Dictionary defines 'enable' as 'to render able; to give power, strength, or competency; to make possible, practical, or easy; and to give the opportunity to'. Whereas such terms come naturally to those involved with management and personal development, they are less clearly associated with the systems analyst, the venture capitalist, the project manager, or the marketing executive. In fact, the person who is most at home with these enabling qualities, is the designer.

HARMONISING yin and yang

The ancient Chinese symbols yin and yang represent complementary 'feminine' and 'masculine' attitudes. Designers, like Mary Quant, have long been aware of the need to balance soft and hard, intuitive and analytical, artistic and scientific capabilities in their work. The principles of design, which deal with balance, are unity and variety, accent and contrast, scale and proportion.

The designer, whether of products or interiors, is interested not only in relations between one material or another, but also between time present and time future. Mary Quant and her husband, Alexander Plunkett Green, could sense that there was a vacuum to be filled after the war. They foresaw the hidden potential. The designer, in fact, is able to give shape to aspirations which all of us possess, but we have not the aptitude to create for ourselves. Mary produced a new 'uniform' for a whole generation, one that they had not been aware they wanted. She was able to turn a strong empathy (yin) for her generation into a clearcut design concept (yang).

The true masters of product design, if not the Italians, are now the Japanese. This is no accident. For the Japanese, whose culture emphasises reciprocal influences, are accustomed to rhythm and balance, accent and contrast. We see it in their famous tea gardens. We also see it in their products. Interestingly enough, Mary Quant has struck up a very strong friendship with her Japanese director. They share an ambiance, an outlook, a sense for true harmony in both products and organisation. There is less in the way of separate identities, more in the way of shared understanding. There is less in the way of product or market segmentation, and more in the way of integration.

> Philosophically yin is female, yang is male. Yin is yielding, while yang represents primal power, energy and strength. Yin is receptive, passive, while yang is dynamic thrusting.[1]

The 'new designer' is primarily yin, but comprehends yang. Meanwhile, the growing interest in yin and yang principles has been accompanied by an increased awareness of the so-called two sides of our brain, to which we now turn.

Recognising the INTUITIVE side of the brain

The growing interest in harmonising yin and yang has been paralleled by recent research into the two sides of the brain. Neurological researchers have discovered that each side of the brain carries with it different kinds of abilities. It so happens that our culture has previously reinforced left brain capacities — analysis, logic, language, at the expense of the right brain functions — intuition, vision, spatial awareness. In the ideal world of organisation and management, both sides should be allowed to fully function. As Marilyn Ferguson, an English writer, resident in America, has said:

> Without the benefit of a scalpel, we perform split-brain surgery on ourselves. We isolate heart and mind. Cut off from the fantasy, the dreams, intuitions and holistic processes of the right brain, the left is sterile. And the right brain, cut off from its organising partner, keeps recycling its emotional charge.[2]

So men label women too emotional, and women label men too impersonal and distant. Organisations become divided, between profit and people, hard attributes and soft ones, formal and informal structures. The 'enabling' function is restricted to soft quarters, somewhere in a personnel enclave, and the rest of the organisation gets on with 'real business'. The hard nosed realists get on with the job while the wide-eyed dreamers look on. Fortunately a design centred organisation, like Mary Quant's has successfully transcended these splits, by maintaining a dynamic balance between product and market, analysis and intuition, man (Alexander) and woman (Mary).

While the right side of the brain has been largely ignored by management students and academics, one man has made a valiant attempt to open our eyes, over the last twenty years. In *The Mechanism of Mind,* written in 1969, Edward De Bono set out his basic theory, that the brain has á pattern making and pattern taking surface:

> Learning is a matter of putting a new pattern onto the surface or changing an established one. Ideally one would let a pattern follow its natural development, and only pay attention to sensitive switch points to make sure that the direction of development was the one required. This would be much more effective than trying to force the pattern onto the surface all the time.[3]

De Bono has compared and contrasted lateral (intuitive) and vertical (analytical) thinking:

> Rightness is what matters in vertical thinking. Richness is what matters in lateral thinking. Vertical thinking selects a pathway by excluding other pathways. Lateral thinking does not select but seeks to open other pathways. With vertical thinking one selects the most promising approach to a problem. With lateral thinking one generates as many alternative approaches as one can.[4]

It is fascinating to see Mary Quant's lateral movement, from stockings and dresses, to hairstyles and cosmetics, from fabrics and household products to printed stationery and published books. For the 'new designer' moves more easily, in a lateral direction, than a vertical one, using the right side of her brain more than the left.

DEVELOPING people and organisations

Unfortunately, a great divide separates those concerned with product design from those versed in organisation development. This is very sad, because the two sides could have so much in common. It is no accident that Mary Quant Ltd. is organised the way it is, with so many lateral connections, and licensing arrangements. The pattern of organisation fits Mary's pattern of thought.

The Council for Art and Industry, in 1937, commented that there is a natural relation between design and the material designed. The design should grow out of the material and be consonant with its qualities and characteristics. It does not require a great leap of imagination to perceive the 'material' as human beings, and the 'design' as the organisation. In fact, Chris Argyris, one of the strongest representatives of the American 'Human Relations' school, has argued, over thirty years, for a closer alignment between individual and organisation:

> Many of the 'human problems' in organisations originally are caused by the basic incongruence between the nature of relatively mature individuals and healthy formal organisations... it follows that effective leadership is 'fusing' the individual and organisation in such a way that both simultaneously obtain self-actualisation.[5]

Argyris has confined himself to traditional ideas on leadership and formal organisation. These might be totally alien to Mary Quant, in her more informal and dispersed working environment. In fact modern exponents of organisation development have paid particular attention to the role of catalyst, facilitator or enabler, rather than to leader. Nancy Foy, in particular, has been preoccupied with the catalytic function, in building bridges between people and organisation. She sees a catalyst as having a well developed sense of design, or aesthetics, as well as being skilled in building 'word pictures' that can be understood across boundaries. But, from then on, the links with the designer become more tenuous. Foy's enabler, or catalyst:

- is aware, sensitive to the need for change and development, and alert to where blockages are likely to be, particularly those which might be turned into helpful energy;

- is a 'social entrepreneur' in that he takes his percentages, as a trader or broker, more in terms of personal development than in financial rewards;
- is a link between inside and outside, one level or function and another, enriching the connective tissue between different entities;
- is a mature outsider, even within his own organisation, and prefers evolution to revolution.

Interestingly enough, Mary Quant strongly exhibits the sensitive awareness, the linkmanship and the maturity that the organisation developer portrays. It is the bridge between 'self' and 'product' development which remains uncrossed. That is why product organisation and business development, have up to now gone separate ways. It is for the 'new designer', as intrapreneur, to cross these boundaries.

SYMBIOSIS through joint ventures

It is no accident that Mary Quant Ltd. has grown through a whole series of licensing agreements with companies large and small. The joint venture in Japan is an extension of that same tendency towards lateral association, rather than vertical integration. Patterns of integration replace hierarchical structures. The designer, enabler, gatekeeper, or catalyst is much more comfortable with these organic, and fluid arrangements, than with the mechanisms of structured organisation, or a fixed product line.

In the last few years, in particular, there has been a spate of joint ventures, not only between designers and manufacturers, but also – and especially – in large scale research projects, in financial services, and in computer hardware and software. Here are just two examples, one from the managing director of Yamaichi Securities Company, which recently opened up in Britain:

The company has taken up a new role as 'financial composer', orchestrating British and Japanese personnel and ideas . . . Japanese, egalitarian style organisation interacting with idiosyncratic British virtues – independence of mind, breadth of view and initiative.[6]

and one from the chief executive of A.T. and T.:

the agreement of Olivetti and A.T. and T. is a major event in the information technology sector, because it unites the complementary strength and capacities of two leading companies for the purpose of establishing an alliance which will play a fundamental role in the development of office automation.[6]

Recognising market COINCIDENCE and potential

In conceiving of a joint venture, the 'new designer' unites the potential of one company with another. In order to do this successfully, she must be able to foresee how they might favourably interconnect. She needs to be able to match the other company's needs against her own.

Similar principles apply, when spotting a market gap, or sensing a need that is going begging. The conventional marketing texts gloss over the intuitive wisdom that is involved in 'feeling' for market trends and potential. It is the kind of wisdom and insight that a commodity dealer or business broker requires, alongside the person who conceives of a new business idea, or potential market.

The qualities required are sensitivity and openness, an ability to connect like with unlike, a willingness to be surprised, a fascination for, and with, coincidence, an interest in how things evolve and develop, and a tendency to see the world, including the market place, as shifting, overlapping and ever changing.

All of these qualities characterise Mary Quant. As a fashion designer she anticipates and forecasts. Her eye keeps finding things in new combinations. A leotard is a body stocking is a vest is underwear. She develops empathy with others, as colleagues and as clients, in Britain or Japan. Luck follows her around and coincidence, as well as surprise, are part and parcel of the visual effect she creates.

Chance and response, between them, provide the warp and woof of her business and the pattern of her life. The external chances of life play upon her, and as she responds to them, she shapes her luck.

Developing communication NETWORKS

The focus on joint venturing and market awareness, as well as the shift from an exclusively competitive thrust to an equally collaborative one, reflects a wide-spread change of emphasis, economically, socially and technologically. It is represented, for one thing, in the emergence of communication networks. As a social phenomenon, Marilyn Ferguson, in her oft quoted book, *Aquarian Conspiracy*, has referred to networks as an important vehicle for personal, business and organisation development. Ferguson argues that the organic, network mode of organisation is more biologically adaptive, more efficient, and more 'conscious' than the hierarchical structure of modern business and civilisation. She maintains that the function of most of these networks is mutual support and enrichment, empowerment of the individual, and co-operation to effect change. Paradoxically, a network is both intimate and expansive. Unlike an hierarchical structure, it can maintain its personal or local quality while ever growing. Networks promote the linkage of their members with other people, other networks, promoting ever greater communication, association and awareness. Whereas a conventional organisation chart would show neatly linked boxes, coalitions of networks look like:

> a badly knotted fishnet with a multitude of nodes of varying sizes, each linked to all the others, directly or indirectly.[7]

Human networks are greatly amplified by their electronic counterparts and vice versa. In business, the 'distributed network', so-called, is becoming common currency. In an article that appeared in the *Financial Times* on 30 March 1984, Rob Wilmott, managing director of ICL, spoke of his company's plans for:

> a networked product line in which each piece of equipment

will be designed to interconnect with both the company's own products and with those of other computer manufacturers.

Technological networks, social networks, as well as business networks create sums much greater than their parts. Mary Quant is part of an enormous business network, connecting suppliers and consumers all over the world, and orchestrated through an intricate set of licensing agreements reinforced by trusting relationships. Hers is very much an 'integrated', or interdependent business organisation.

Conclusion

One of the wisest business academics of our time, the Dutchman Bernard Lievegoed, claims that organisations go through three stages of development. The first, pioneering stage is 'entrepreneurial'. The second, consolidating one is 'managerial'. The third, mature stage, he calls 'integrated':

> If we start with the entrepreneurial initiative of the pioneer as our thesis, then scientific management is in a certain sense the antithesis and a third step will have to be the synthesis.[8]

In this third stage, the emphasis is upon evolution, interdependence, and integration – economically, socially and technologically. As a result the 'new designer' gains prominence, as organisation developer, 'financial composer', market gatekeeper or even business strategist. It is her function, in one capacity or another, to create synergy, to stimulate interdependence, to think laterally. She recognises human and market potential, observes patterns of evolution, facilitates business and organisational change, and, above all, enables development to occur.

References

1   Colegrave, S., *The Spirit of the Valley*, Virago Press, London, 1979.
2   Ferguson, M., *The Aquarian Conspiracy*, Granada, London, 1980.

3 De Bono, E., *The Mechanism of Mind*, Jonathan Cape, London, 1969.
4 De Bono, E., *Lateral Thinking*, Penguin Books, Harmondsworth, 1977.
5 Argyris, C., *Personality and Organisation*, Harper and Row, London, 1957.
6 *Financial Times*, January 17, 1984.
7 Ferguson, M., *The Aquarian Conspiracy*, Granada, London, 1980.
8 Lievegoed, B., *The Developing Organisation*, Tavistock, London, 1973.

Providing structure – John Harvey Jones, leader

5

> What I want to create is an adaptive company that has got some of the values you need to survive in tomorrow's world... by the year 2000, we need to become the chemical problem solvers of the world.
>
> Sir John Harvey Jones, Chairman, ICI

I was born in London, but spent my early years in India. My father was a professional prime minister! He was hired by an Indian state to run its affairs, and I was brought up with the Maharaja almost as an elder brother.

When still very young I was brought over to this country and dumped in a British prep school in Kent. It was notable for its building, and I hated it. I was basically unequipped to cope. Other boys had homes to go to, and I was on my own. I vividly remember a friend going home for his fifth birthday, and there was I... I survived with difficulty.

The school was, basically, a middle-class crammer, and one thing it did do was to teach you how to concentrate and work. I've never believed in all this inspirational stuff. It's the 90 per cent perspiration that really counts. So I did reasonably well at school, through effort. I wasn't intellectually clever.

After school, I decided to go into the navy. Law was my first choice, but my parents couldn't afford it. I decided I ought to earn a living. I was attracted by a life of adventure.

I was a great reader. C.S. Forester and that type of thing. I still love those books. Perhaps I've never grown up.

Anyway, *I went on to Dartmouth naval college. The discipline was draconian. I loved it. It was a totally institutionalised set up.* They didn't educate you. You were trained. They barely attempted, for example, to teach you economic history as a discipline in its own right. You merely learnt about Nelson's battles of the Nile. What they were trying to do was to set a high standard for failed officers.

I was reasonably strong academically. In the top ten. But I never became a leading scholar. I was interested in English and in languages. I was able to join a so called 'alpha' university class. It was pathetic but genuine. I also did French, German and History. The trouble with the sciences, on the other hand, was that you only did naval things.

When I finished at College, I went to sea. It was during the war, and I was under 17. We were sunk a couple of times before I was 18. I became a sub-lieutenant specialising in the submarine service. After the war was over, the submarine I joined was in a mess, in fact so much so that the first 8 months of peace were more dangerous than ever.

At the time they were looking for volunteers to learn Russian. The bait was Cambridge. I had always wanted to go to university. I wanted to go to Cambridge and have a good time. But it wasn't to be.

My submarine experience did a lot of things for me. There was rigorous discipline, but it wasn't hierarchical. We all worked in close proximity. There was a high degree of mutual respect. After all, we were all capable of sinking the sub. So it was friendly and un-institutionalised. The discipline was real, but we mucked in together, officers and men. It was a team thing. This had a profound effect. It taught me that the difference between individuals is marginal. It's basically the luck of the draw. Everyone has the same difficulties.

That's where my left-wing predilections emerged from. The background and conditions of the sailors touched me deeply. The unequal society raised its ugly head. I'm still in touch with some of the sailors to this day.

Meanwhile, at Cambridge I had to learn Russian, rather than having a good time. The lady professor had a contract with the navy to teach us, and we were a trial batch. So she took it very seriously. For three weeks there was a battle of wills, and those that survived learnt Russian. It was difficult to sit down and think, after being in the submarine service, when all you did was react.

I then went on to do a civil service interpretership. I did jobs with naval intelligence, using my Russian. I was then pulled back and put into the Cabinet Office because of the experience I had had with Russians, during my eighteen months of intelligence work. For the first time I came into contact with the workings of government, and with the really top brass. People like Montgomery. I always envisaged the top brass doing these really big jobs, but I was quickly disillusioned. After one or two weeks in the Cabinet Office I was asked to draw·up the British strategy for a matter of great importance. I knew virtually nothing about it, and just used my common sense. When the thing came bouncing back, I expected to have to completely re-draft it. All I got back was spelling mistakes!

I did see the workings of government, then, at first hand. What was most important was how much I discovered about what wasn't done. Then I was sent off to occupied Germany. It was 1946.

Germany was in an appalling state at the time. There was death and starvation in the streets. The whole of society had collapsed. Family life had disintegrated. It was very nasty.

I lived and worked close at hand with the Russians. I then went back to the Cabinet Office. I also got married. I love my wife very deeply. In fact I not only love her, but I also like her. At first I made the running, but now it's a mutual passion. I'm bloody lucky.

After two years I went back to Germany. 1949. I did a series of intelligence assignments. I was naval officer in charge of Kiel, on the Baltic, and then Hamburg. I worked primarily with Germans, commanding one of their vessels. That was interesting. I was given a pot of money to set things up, and left to get on with it, not being given any guidance. Living in, and running a German ship, taught me a great deal about another different country. Although German discipline can be draconian, I made sure that we ran the thing as a team, with mutual respect amongst officers and men.

I was given the MBE for the period, and was very proud of it. We did a number of naughty things! Then it was decided I needed a rest.

I was sent off to the Far East. The Korean War was going on at the time. It was not much of a rest. People were killing each other all over the place.

We then went off to the Antarctic. That was a fascinating experience.

Just before I left for Korea my daughter was born. She was six weeks old when I went off. I didn't see her again until three years later. It had a profound effect on my relationship with her. It's alright now, but it took a long time to heal. She was so close to her ma.

When I came back from the Antarctic, I was put into the Admiralty, to do another intelligence job. I was there a year when my daughter got polio. A year later it became apparent that she would recover the use of her legs. She has been in leg irons since, and in continual pain. It's been a bloody hard life for her.

I concluded I couldn't go on globetrotting. It was too disruptive of family life. I had become a rare kind in the Navy, with my specialised knowledge in Russian. There were only four others like me. But I wanted a nine to five job, to keep me at home.

At that time, *I stopped wanting to have a career.* I had had a very good one. And that was it.

I selected ICI for my new job, then, for three reasons. My brother-in-law had joined, and he loved it. Two other friends had left the navy to join ICI, and one said he'd get me an interview. Thirdly, I believed England was heading for an economic mess. *I felt the need to get into something basic. I had a need to perform a service. Something socially responsible. I'm not driven by money, and never have been.* I won't do a thing for money.

I know what makes me run. I thought industry had a social role. And what makes me run is achievement. I need to live up to my own standards. My cardinal sin is pride. Self pride. I don't care what other people say about me, but I care what I think about myself. *I know what I think a 'man' ought to do. I have this inner compulsion. I have to perform, and to ensure that I can make things happen.* I must feel that something has my name tag, for me to see and nobody else.

I'll give an example. There's a refinery in Teesside. I know that it only exists because it was a concept I created, a deal I put together. It's still there. Every time I go near it, and take a look, I feel great. It's still running, still employing people. To see it gives me an inner satisfaction worth a guinea a box. It hasn't changed the face of the world, but it has given me the satisfaction of a creation that's working. I'm not interested in calling it the Harvey Jones works. I know what I did. I know the struggle. I know the deals.

There's another example. *In 1957 the company tried to introduce a new agreement on the Wilton Works. At the time we'd lost control of the place.* There was a strong group of shop stewards. Anyway, *I was put into Wilton, to resolve the problem.* There was a united shop stewardry. Management never dared confront them. It was a crucial site, and confrontation could have been incredibly expensive. *A flare up would bring the whole site down. Nobody on the management side dared stand his ground.*

Management has to have some credibility. You need a power balance. The problem is to create that balance, and hold it enough to create genuine linkage between the two sides. It was a long and traumatic time for me. I had to take some strikes and win them, but ensure that they didn't last for more than two or three days. I had to choose my ground carefully. *I had to unite the management. I set up the largest training exercise that had ever been undertaken in ICI. 2000 people were sent on a Coverdale management course. I didn't care what course they did as long as it built up a team spirit.*

When I took the job over, there was not a single manager from Wilton on an ICI Divisional Board. The site was operating poorly. I had to get it back. I knew my name plate was on it, and I wanted to achieve results without changing the management.

Today, it's one of the best run sites, and many of the

managers have moved on to high positions. Wilton now compares favourably with anywhere in the world. I was back there last Friday. It's marvellous to see. Of course, at the time when I was there, process planning, joint problem solving and joint teamwork was revolutionary, long-haired and way out!

Now let me go back to the beginning, at least of my ICI days. I joined the works study department as the lowest example of a manager. I spent the first years trying to find out what a manager was. I was very naive about industry, and very poorly paid. In the navy I had been getting £1700 per annum, and at ICI I started on £800. I've always had tremendous prospects and no money! Because I started on such a low financial ebb, my increments since that time have always been based on that low point. It's ludicrous. And I since found out that I could have asked for more when I started.

Thankfully I soon got sent on to Wilton. It was run by a service organisation at the time. I was fairly quickly moved on from being a stop-watch banger on to night shifts. They were marvellous.

My wife initially stayed on in London. Again, in my naïveté, I worked all hours. My very first job was to study an incinerator. You couldn't see it for piles of muck. I was told to do a method study. I found out that the guys just weren't putting the stuff into the incinerator. I spent three days there, eighteen hours a day. Then I went back to the boss, and told him he wouldn't need another incinerator. He told me to go back and do the job properly. But there was nothing more to do, so I spent ten happy days as a stoker with the boys. Then I submitted the same report, with just a change of date.

At that time I was working night shift with the troops. Most companies are completely different at night. During the night things just work, with the minimum of people and fuss. During the day you have the whole panoply of power!

I became a section manager, and continued to starve! I have a theory about money. There's a level below which you have no disposable income. Once my wife and I were doing the gardening, and we pulled out this old rake. We had to save for three months, back then, just to buy a garden rake.

Anyway, being a Section Manager, for me at that time, was a marvellous job. I had a lot of junior staff and a discreet job to do. I became deputy supplies officer, and had a tremendous time. I still get letters from men and women who worked for me then. It was all about productivity and leadership. Every damn year we reduced our numbers. But we did it nicely, through natural wastage. It was a time of dynamic change in the supply world. John Garnett, at the Industrial Society, claims that the 'briefing groups' idea came from me. Anyway, I set it up. I sat down with all my sections and discussed things with them.

Then Wilton was taken over. It was traumatic. It taught me a great deal about how not to do things. All of our top brass was shunted off, or fired. It was unprecedented for ICI. Wilton was taken over by the Heavy Organic Chemicals Division. I was the only Wilton man given promotion. It wasn't a deliberate choice. I was your token someone! I became supply manager, in any case, for both Wilton and Heavy Organics. It was one of the least important jobs around, given to some erk!

I had 150 people in my department. Heavy Organics had twelve. We combined together under my leadership. The supply role in fact proved extremely important. In Petrochemicals, 50 per cent of the costs go into feedstock. I figured that it could be bought in cheaper. I was sent round the world, on a fact finding mission, and I concluded that we were paying far too much.

I recommended that we build our own refinery. I was sent out to find a contractor, and we got the refinery built. That broke the naphtha price, at least for a while. We then created two selling organisations, and I was put in charge of one, hydrocarbons. That's the time I'm least proud of.

I've never been ambitious. I only wanted to get things done. I never cared a damn about promotion. But I had just this short period when I thought I could get to the Division Board. Yet, it was unthinkable for a non-technologist like me to have the top job.

At the time I thought I could be commercial director.

That was an aberration. When I had left the Service, I was completely freed of ambition. My career was over. Since then, I've been totally committed to telling the truth, as I saw it. I never play politics. I never scheme, unless it is in order to make something happen. Yet, in that short period I did become political, for my own sake. My wife saved me from continuing along that road, and I have never done it since.

They did put me on the Board, in this techno-commercial job. After that, I became Wilton's Personnel Director. Within a year the Deputy Chairman's role became vacant. I was the only guy around at the time, so I got the job. It had been the same with the personnel job. I got into both by default! I managed to manage, but I was moved on too quickly. I took over from the old guard, and when I left it was handed over to them. There was no continuity.

I was amazed to be appointed Division Chairman. I was given a clear-up job. The business base wasn't sound enough when I took over. In the first year I was there we only avoided making a loss by selling off our waste heat. In my three years there, though, I doubled the profits every year. I was also ordered to amalgamate Wilton and Fibres. Today the two together are one third the size that Petrochemicals had been.

I created a new outfit, with a new identity. That's the art of amalgamation, to create a third, and completely new entity, rather than have one company take over another. If you go to petrochemicals now, people wouldn't remember whether they were originally this division or that. Then I was put on the Main Board.

Initially, *I was put in charge of Organisation. I made three attempts to change the way the Board did its business.* The first one got me a bloody nose. The other two achieved a bit. *In fact, the way the Board operated hadn't changed for yonks, since Chambers' day.* It had grown up its collectivist approach, as a reaction against the power mongering of McGowan and Chambers.

I'm a strong believer in group leadership but not in consensus. My job is to manage the Board, and to make sure it makes decisions. I have to polarise things. Good boards don't operate on a basis of no conflict. But, no way do I want people to row, and to hate each other. Argument there must be, but good humoured stuff. I'll listen and change if I can't carry people. If anyone is bypassed, then they still must be heard. They must have a kick at the ball. And if things turn out wrong for me, I shall always say, 'Well Alan and Charles did say this might happen.'

What I want to create is an adaptive company that has got some of the values you need, to survive in tomorrow's world. I believe passionately that you should not have any organisation layers, unless they visibly add to the party. The Board's job, meanwhile, should be unique. It is concerned more with the what than the how. When you mix the two you get into trouble. The art of jacking any business up is continuously to set people targets, a bit beyond their perceived capability, and then ensure they achieve them.

We need to become the chemical problem solvers of the world, by the year 2000. Whenever you have a chemistry problem, you ring up ICI, and, of course, we get paid for it. We're not doing good for love. But our customers must profit from working with us.

I envisage that when I've done this job, I'll retire and do something with my family. By the time I'm done, I'll be knackered. I give this job everything I've got. I'll be ashamed if I'm bounding with vigour at the end of it. I think I'm leading the best large company in the country, but neither my wife nor I get our pleasures from driving a Rolls or having lunch with Maggie.

We have an eleven-year-old granddaughter now. She's lovely. I teach her how to swim. I'm a total believer in people. It's like a lot of things in life. You get what you expect, and you get back what you give. The job of leader is to get extraordinary performances out of ordinary people. There's no achievement in taking over a company, firing everybody, and bringing in seven whizz kids. That's not my style. I like to build the leaders I've got, to be leaders.

I often do reflect on what I have done. I'm not self obsessed, but I do spend a tremendous amount of time trying to analyse what is happening, in human relations terms. Nine times out of ten, I kill the problem, or else I'm in the wrong job!

****
Providing structure
****

– the emergence of **bureaucracy**

from ancient Egypt, through China, the Roman Empire and unto today

– introducing measurement and **control**

through the 'invention' of a 'science' of management

– specifying managerial **functions**

which cover business operations as well as managerial activities

– outlining the **concept** of the business

whereby the product, market and business mission is defined

– focusing on the organisation **structure**

encompassing both the formal structure and the social organisation

– introducing **systems** theory

through which inputs are transformed into outputs

– **co-ordinating** managerial work

by combining the 'hard' and 'soft' elements of managerial activity

– business as **service**

fulfilling the needs of society through the products of the business

– providing **direction**

by infusing purpose and lending perspective

****

bureaucracy – are the operations efficient?

- What clearly defined laws, rules and principles have been established?
- Is activity clearly segmented along functional lines, creating specialised production, marketing, finance and personnel activity?

control – is there self-mastery and institutional control?

- Are there policies, programmes and procedures to cover all important matters?
- Are there controls to compel events to conform to plan?

function – is each part of the organisation functioning effectively?

- Are production, marketing, financial and personnel functions installed, maintained and developed?
- Are the basic functions of management – planning, organising, directing and control – operational?

concept

- Is there a clear understanding of policies, strategies, and programmes of activity?
- Is the business product and mission clearly conceptualised and communicated?

71

structure – does everyone know their place?

- Is there a clearly structured hierarchy of authority?
- Has a structure of roles been established at different levels of the organisation?

system – are the parts integrated within the whole?

- Is the organisation functioning effectively as an overall, interdependent system?
- Are the sub-systems – technical, social, structural and managerial – operating efficiently?

co-ordination – is there a good balance of 'soft' and 'hard' qualities?

- Are there good lines of communication throughout?
- Is there effective co-operation between people?

service

- What service is the business providing its customers?
- How is society being served?

direction – does everybody know where they are going?

- Does the company know what business it is in, could be in, should be in?
- Have clear objectives been set at all levels, and in all businesses and functions?

****

Whereas 'designers' can sense and stimulate potential, managers are adept at channelling it. From the time that business enterprises became structured into formal entities, with distinct functions and delegated responsibilities, managers came into their own. If we trace the origins of ICI, for example, its two founding fathers were Alfred Nobel and Ludwig Mond, both innovative scientists. It was Mond's son, Alfred, who was first able to articulate the functions of management and organisation. He was not a scientist in his own right but more of a leader and statesman. John Harvey Jones has emerged out of the Alfred Mond tradition, but brings a contemporary ring to his style of leadership. John also draws on a now established tradition of management, which did not exist in his predecessor's time.

The great advantage of management, is that it can be conceptualised, put into words, communicated easily to others, and taught precisely, in classroom situations. It can be neatly abstracted from the hurly burly of everyday experience, and codified in management texts. Both as a specialist and generalist subject, it is taught around the business schools of the world. Production, marketing, financial and personnel management have become part of college curricula in Britain, Europe, America and in Commonwealth countries. General management and business policy have gained equal popularity throughout the universities and polytechnics. So what is management, and how has it evolved over time?

Early contributions to management principles

THE EMERGENCE OF 'BUREAUCRACY'

Interpretations of early Egyptian papyri, extending as far back as 1300 BC, reflect the importance of organisation and administration in the bureaucratic states of antiquity. Similar records exist for China, where Confucius' parables include practical suggestions for public administration. In ancient Greece, Socrates defined management as a skill, apart from technical knowledge and experience, in a way that is reminiscent of modern practice. Through the use of scalar principles of organisation, and the delegation of authority, ancient Rome was expanded to an empire with an efficiency of organisation never before observed.

It was this efficiency and discipline in the 'institutionalised set up' at naval college, that Harvey Jones loved in his youth. Together with efficiency in organisation, comes a scientific approach to management.

INTRODUCING MEASUREMENT AND 'CONTROL'

The so called founder of 'scientific management' was the American, Frederick W. Taylor. He came to prominence at a time, in the 1900s, when the rise of large scale industry and the introduction of expensive machinery, called for skilled managers. Hence Taylor, in America, developed his *Principles of Scientific Management:*

> First: To point out the great loss which the whole country is suffering through inefficiency in almost all of our daily acts.
> Second: To try to convince the reader that the remedy for this inefficiency lies in systematic management, rather than in searching for some extraordinary man.
> Third: To prove that the best management is a true science, resting upon clearly defined laws, rules and principles.[1]

Taylor was a pioneer in developing approaches to the 'scientific' selection and training of workmen, and the sub-division of jobs and tasks. But the real founder of modern management theory was the French industrialist, Henri Fayol. The Frenchman wrote as the practical man of business reflecting on his long managerial career and setting down the principles he observed. Fayol found that all activities of industrial undertaking could be divided into six groups: (1) technical (production); (2) commercial (buying, selling and exchange); (3) finance (search for, and optimal use of capital); (4) security (protection of property and persons); (5) accounting (including statistics); (6) managerial (planning, organisation, command, co-ordination, and control). These very functions still characterise ICI's management structure today. (The only real omission was 'personnel', which Fayol conceptualised as 'security', including protection of property and persons.)

The evolution of modern management

SPECIFYING MANAGERIAL FUNCTIONS

Fayol's principles, first introduced in Britain and America in the 1930s, were extended and developed by Peter Drucker. Drucker has drawn on both the commercial and the managerial aspects of Fayol's work, in the 1940s and 1950s. In contemporary writings he still refers to the five basic 'operations',[2] in the work of the manager; (1) the setting of objectives, (2) organisation and the analysis of activities; (3) motivation and communication, (4) measurement and control, and (5) the development of people. This is very much a variation on Fayol's basic theme, with perhaps a greater emphasis on people and their development. It is this emphasis on the development of people which so much characterises Harvey Jones' style of leadership.

THE CONCEPT OF BUSINESS

Henri Fayol not only laid the foundations for management principles, but also for business policy and administration. Once again the redoubtable Peter Drucker picked up Fayol's loose threads, conceptualised business per se, and started up the 'Business Policy' tradition.

For Drucker:

> Not intuition, but a clear, simple and penetrating theory of the business characterises the truly successful entrepreneur, the person who not just amasses a large fortune, but builds an organisation that can endure and grow.[2]

The individual entrepreneur starting up in business – like Alfred Nobel – has no need for a clearly articulated business concept. His product is clearcut, and his drives are largely subconscious. The managed enterprise, however, demands a clear definition of business purpose or mission. Here Drucker spells out his three famous questions, which all good students of business policy are invited to ask – What business are we in? What business could we be in? What business should we be in?

Today, as a managed organisation, ICI has to address these questions. Its emerging business is 'chemical problem solving', and Harvey Jones is intent on creating an adaptive company that has some of the values ICI needs to survive in tomorrow's world.

THE ORGANISATION 'STRUCTURE'

It is the theory of 'organisation', rather than the theory of 'business' which has captured the minds, if not the hearts, of management analysts over the years. For while business, as a whole, remained closely identified with the illusive entrepreneur, organisation was very closely linked with management.

The organisational tradition, aside from its longstanding origins in ancient Egypt, China, Greece and Rome, draws more recently on the work of the German sociologist, Max Weber, who in the nineteenth century, saw the need to depersonalise a sometimes corrupt and often exploitative system of production:

> Its development has created an urgent need for stable, strict, intensive and capable administration. It is this need which gives bureaucracy a crucial role in our society, as the central element in any large scale administration.[3]

Weber then went on to identify nine characteristics of bureaucratic organisations:

- personally free
- organised in a clearly defined hierarchy
- each office has a clearly defined sphere of competence
- free selection of people
- people selected on the basis of technical competence
- almost fixed tenure
- allowing career promotion
- separation of ownership from control
- subject to discipline

His intentions were to organise for freedom from arbitrary authority, which was very appropriate for the time. In more recent years, bureaucracy has assumed rather different proportions. While most large organisations continue to have clearly delineated structures of authority and control, these are becoming increasingly inconsistent with the need for individual self-expression and market responsiveness.

However, the theory of organisation has not been restricted to the concept of 'bureaucracy'. In fact, as a direct reaction against Weber's hierarchical principles and Taylor's 'scientific management', the 'human relations' movement was born in America, in the 1940s. Elton Mayo, one of its pioneers, put it this way, just after the war:

> Effective co-operation is the problem we face in the middle of the twentieth century. I believe that social study should begin with careful observation of what may be described as communication: that is, the capacity of an individual to communicate his feelings and ideas to another, the capacity of groups to communicate effectively and intimately with each other. This issue is, beyond all reasonable doubt, the outstanding defect that civilisation faces today.[4]

So with Mayo, we move away from emphasis upon structure and organisation toward people and communication. Harvey Jones has been concerned not with one or the other, but with both, at ICI. An even more recent development has been to concentrate on organisations as 'open systems'.

For the systems theorists, organisations are viewed as social and technical systems, composed of a number of subsystems. They receive inputs of energy, information and materials from the environment, transforming these, and returning outputs to the environment.

The organisation's goals and values are one of the more important of these subsystems. The organisation performs a function for society, and if it is to be successful in receiving inputs, it must conform to social requirements. The 'technical' subsystem refers to the knowledge required in the performance of tasks, including the techniques used in the transformation of inputs into outputs. Every organisation also has a 'psychosocial' subsystem which is composed of individuals and groups in interaction, as well as a 'structural' one, through which its tasks are divided and co-ordinated. Finally, the 'managerial' subsystem spans the entire organisation, by relating the institution to its environment, setting the goals, developing comprehensive, strategic, and operational plans, designing the structure, and establishing the control process.

The functioning of the ICI Board, as Harvey Jones now sees it, is consistent with this comprehensive, strategic, systematic approach.

CO-ORDINATING MANAGERIAL WORK

Theories of organisation and management have had a strong conceptual base, as have the management principles that preceded them. In recent years, the applicability of these theories, to the practical world of management, has come into question. A provocative article appeared in the McKinsey Quarterly of Spring 1976 entitled *What Managers Do: fact and folklore*.[5] Its author, a Canadian by the name of Mintzberg, had spent several years studying senior managers in action.

His conclusion was that such operations as planning, organising and control were not particularly useful, as a way of categorising live management. The divisions he came up with were those shown below, with decision making, interpersonal contacts, and information processing as the major categories:

MANAGERIAL WORK

Decision making	Information processing	Interpersonal contacts
– disturbance handling – negotiation – resource allocation	– monitor – nerve centre – disseminator	– liaison – leader – figurehead

The flavour of Mintzberg's divisions is very different from Fayol's or even Peter Drucker's. They are more varied, more full of imagery, more personal, and generally more practical. Disturbance handling and liaison activity for example, are more immediate and visible than planning and control. At the same time, his three major divisions do remain completely divided one from the other.

This analytical divisiveness is exactly what has come under fire in the American best seller *In Search of Excellence:*

> Underscoring the whole problem may be a missing perspective, the lack of any feeling for the whole on the part of the so called professional manager.[6]

Peters and Waterman have criticised the over-emphasis on rational organisation and management. Instead, they have come up with a balance of soft (shared values, style, skills and staff) and hard (strategy, structure and systems) qualities. In the interests of wholeness, Peters and Waterman have substituted 'excellence' for efficiency and effectiveness. The excellent manager in fact:

- is adept at managing ambiguity and paradox
- has a bias for action
- is close to the customer
- encourages autonomy and entrepreneurship
- achieves productivity through people
- is hands on, value driven
- sticks to the knitting (the core of the business)
- has a simple organisational form, and a lean staff.

Harvey Jones, as ICI's leader, has visibly encouraged autonomy and entrepreneurship, while demonstrating a bias for action and bringing the company closer to the customer. Most particularly and consistently, though, over the years, he has focused on raising productivity through his concern for people.

Conclusion

BUSINESS AS SERVICE

Before concluding this section of management, I want to go back to Henry Ford, the founding father, not of management theory, but of business philosophy. On the one hand, Ford, through his company and his work methods, brought out the best and the worst of scientific management.

On the other hand, Henry Ford had a great deal to say about the function of business, as a service. For it was the purpose of business, he emphasised, to produce for consumption and not for money or speculation. Capital is for the service of all, he said, though it might be under the direction of one. The highest use of capital was not to make more money, but to make money do more service for the betterment of life. Unless, he felt, industries were helping to solve social and economic problems, they would not be fulfilling their proper function. In that context Ford is expressing beliefs not at all dissimilar from those of John Harvey Jones, who wants ICI to become the chemical problem solver of the world. In that wide-ranging capacity, John is providing the company with a new direction.

PROVIDING DIRECTION

In the last one or two years there has been a renewed interest in 'leadership', as opposed to the more impersonal 'management'. For Harvey Jones, the essence of leadership is 'to get extraordinary performances out of ordinary people'.

The literature on leadership is not always helpful in enabling us to differentiate between manager and leader. Often it resorts to mere platitudes. However, Alistair Mant, in his recent book *Leaders we Deserve,* introduces the useful idea of 'tripodal'   , as opposed to 'bi-podal'   , leadership.

In other words, the true leader serves a cause that transcends mere survival (us versus them) or even productivity (profit versus people). That cause may be written into the business' constitution or else represented through its products. ICI, as a company, is chemically driven. And John Harvey Jones, as a leader, is transforming it from a company that was responsible, but resistant to change, into one that is not only responsible but also responsive and adaptable.

What, in fact, distinguishes Harvey Jones from the more conventional business executive, is that he infuses ICI with purpose and direction. He therefore rises above the more impersonal aspects of management, without discarding them. He becomes master of the company bureaucracy rather than being subservient to it. He uses measurement and control to stretch his people, rather than to constrain them. The functions of management, at least within his Board, are integrated rather than separated. Harvey Jones has a clear concept of where ICI has come from, and where the business is going.

In focusing on the organisation structure in general, and his Board in particular, ICI's Chairman has put a premium on both autonomy for the Divisions, and on wholeness, at the top. He is very conscious of the part ICI plays in society, as a subsystem of a wider system. The company has not only become more responsive to its stakeholders — particularly its customers — since Harvey Jones took over, but it also sees its products as serving the needs of the community at large.

Above all, Harvey Jones has been able to combine the soft and hard qualities of management, as his life history makes so apparent. He is that rare combination of hard nosed and profit oriented, on the one hand, and soft-hearted and socially sensitive, on the other. Structure and authority combine with empathy and camaraderie in Harvey Jones' world. He infuses, and is infused with, direction.

References

1   Taylor, F.W., *The Principles of Scientific Management,* Harper & Brothers, 1911.
2   Drucker, P., *Management: tasks, responsibilities, practices,* Pan Books, 1979.
3   Weber, M., ex Pugh, D., *Writers on Organisations,* Penguin Books, Harmondsworth, 1972.
4   Mayo, E., *The Social Problem of an Industrial Civilisation,* Routledge and Kegan Paul, London, 1949.
5   Mintzberg, H., 'What Managers Do: fact and folklore', *McKinsey Quarterly,* Spring, 1976.
6   Peters, T. and Waterman, R. *In Search of Excellence,* Harper and Row, London, 1982.

Acquiring resources – Jack Dangoor, entrepreneur

6

> Money is of no interest to me. It's the beauty of having done it at 28. To do it and remain so small delights me. We want to be the people who put a computer on everyone's desk, while retaining a low profile.
>
> Jack Dangoor, Advance Technology

I have an excellent memory, almost a photographic one in fact. I can remember my childhood in Iraq very clearly. Just before we emigrated to England, we had returned home from a European trip. President Kassim was in power. There were 200 000 Jews in Iraq. As a good, propaganda-oriented society, we were given tons of free books. A few days after we returned there was a coup. We burnt Kassim's books. The very same evening he and his aides were killed. I clearly remember seeing Zorro on TV at home. The film was interrupted. They showed us a newsreel of the previous regime, all with their throats cut. I was seven at the time. You know, the Jews were the first people to inhabit Iraq. Now the population has gone down from 200 000 to 150.

I was at school till eighteen, and did my 'A' levels in maths and physics. I went on to London University to study physics, and left after 2 years. I don't know why. I had just had enough. At university they point you in a certain direction, and that wasn't mine.

I joined my father's wholesaling business and started the

81

watch department which grew to quite a large size. But I had an argument, after two years, with my father's partners. Rather than fighting I decided to leave. I was twenty three.

It is difficult to say what one picks up along the way. It just comes. I'm a profuse reader of business magazines. Fifteen a week. *Fortune, Business Week, Investor's Chronicle.* I just love reading them. If I see a magazine with an attractive cover, and biotechnology written on it, I'll buy it. I don't read many books. I lack the interest span. But I love spy stories, especially to read on the plane. I used to fly to Hong Kong seven times a year.

When I left the family business, people still used to 'phone me in the morning and ask when I was coming in. They could not believe I had left. But I decided I would start my own business, and in what I knew best, watches. I borrowed £500 from my sister, not to be beholden to my father. His partners tried to stop me from setting up, but they couldn't.

The secret of my business was that small buyers could only buy from small sellers, and the large buyers only bought from large ones. If I want to open a small shop, to make computers in my back street, I can sell to a small company. But to sell to a large company, you need large scale production. So I stepped in between, and bought up large batches of watches, from Switzerland and Hong Kong, to serve large retailers. I could do it because I knew what would sell.

I started by renting a little place, though I had no money to pay the first quarter's rent. I did my own letterheads with the address I was hoping to move into, and had my ansaphone at home. I went to Hong Kong and arranged with my previous suppliers to sell to me. Through financial fast footwork, we somehow survived and flourished. Watches had a product life of three months. The prices fell from £250 to £3. You had to have a good feel for what was coming and going. To acquire that feel, you had to do a lot of legwork, going to visit the factories to find out what the competition would be doing tomorrow. The similarities between the watch and computer businesses are staggering.

In both markets, the bottom gets crunched first. You have the bottom, the middle and the top. The top pushes down, and becomes almost indistinguishable from the middle. The machines under £200 are suffering most erosion. But what will really hurt is when the top end, like IBM, reduce their PC to £1000. The middle is very much dependent on the top.

The thing is, the people who buy the lowest cost product do it for low cost, not for performance. If you're interested in a keyboard and a particular memory capacity, you'll buy the cheapest, like the Spectrum. It won't matter if the Oric has better sound or graphics. Now, it takes a lot of money for the manufacturer to develop the higher priced machine. So the people who are capable of producing and mass marketing are the larger companies, with larger overheads. For example, ACT must have required £30 million to produce their Apricot. And if it costs £1000 per unit to build, they add on overheads and profit margin, which brings it up to £3000. Meanwhile, the middle market doesn't need the sophistication. It uses simpler, more standard items, therefore reducing the company's entry price. If it costs them £250 to make, they can sell for £500.

So the top end is at a disadvantage, what with their heavy overheads. On the other hand they have the reserves. So when the competition gets hot they can outlast all comers. We used to buy identical products to Time Products, and sell for £15 what they sold for £30. Eventually they had to cut their prices, and in the end they lost their shirts, but we lost our whole business. The lesson I learnt is that you need to be best in both worlds, large and nimble on your feet.

Although we were ultimately forced out, it was a voluntary decision on our part, before the real crunch came. Around 1982, we'd already become the distributor for Sanyo watches in the UK. We took it on because it gave us an introduction into markets where we had previously not been welcomed. The really large buyers had not wanted to know us. But once we had the Sanyo business they were interested.

I had met the MD of Sanyo, in Hong Kong, by sheer coincidence. We got their business in a week, though people had told us it would take two to three years. Meanwhile, we had to find another product. The writing was on the wall for us in watches. We neither had the money nor the inclination to stay the long term.

IBM had just entered the personal computer market in 1982. It was obvious to me that they were going to dominate it. That meant more software would be produced for their computer than for any other. I decided, then, that we had to get into computers, and that the machine had to be IBM compatible. I discovered that there was nothing else, at the time, on the market. So we had to produce our own.

We had a very long way to go. We were totally unrespectable. So I had to surround myself with respectability. The only way was to hide myself and to try and project an image of something the final customer would like to see. The respectable manufacturers in UK were Marconi, Plessey and Ferranti.

After we'd decided to develop our own computer, I came across this so-called ULA technology. What it means is that you can make a few custom components instead of many standard parts. I discovered this when I first came across Ferranti, who were making a chip for a radio watch. They told me about this fantastic technology they had. You could take a whole board of chips and make it into one. Ferranti were world leaders in ULA technology.

I had realised already that it is easy to make money when market conditions are strong. It is more difficult to survive and prosper when market conditions become disastrous. And that time comes to every market. So I began to organise things, in my mind, so that when the tough times came along, the company would survive.

I started by employing outside consultants to design a machine. From the start, therefore, I had no overheads of my own. I called up the Design Council and asked them for their list of industrial designers. Consultants, in this country, at least those in the electronics design field, are usually people who used to work for large companies. They set up a commune and share the profit. It's a mixture of idealism and financial common sense. They're not funded by private industry, as in America, so they have to earn their fees.

So, besides my industrial designer, I needed an electronics one. Again I got an approved list from the Department of Industry, produced a short list of those who seemed to know something, and then took a pin! By this stage, we knew what we wanted – something like the IBM, but with better performance, and much cheaper. We had endless meetings with the designers and the chip suppliers. The product the designers first came up with would have included supplies that are now horrendously difficult to get. All in all it took a year, spread over two years because of the stop-go, while we looked around for more funds. We only went full steam ahead, though, once we had secured promises of orders.

We produced a model, a specification and a price and went round to prospective customers. I decided to go for the export markets first. If you go into a UK retail store, you have to plonk your machine on the table, prepared to deliver immediately. Importers, on the other hand, are used to seeing the product at an advance stage. So we wrote to literally everybody overseas we could get hold of. I went to Chambers of Commerce, Boards of Trade and got loads of addresses. We asked for lists of anybody who may be interested, picking a whole block of countries round the world at a time.

By this time I had brought my brother-in-law in, on the sales side. We mailed a simple photocopy of the product plus the specification and price. This was well before the quantum leap, Sinclair's product, came to light. Ours is not an innovation. We converted a product, which could be made by a big company, into a cheaper, higher performing, equivalent.

We got quite a few enquiries coming back, given that our price was one third that of the IBM personal computer. Eventually we had prospective orders for thousands of machines. So it was like a ballet. Our customers would only place firm orders if we could commit Ferranti to manufacture. Ferranti would only commit themselves, once we had firm orders. Eventually we got the orders placed, provided Ferranti would manufacture. They came from Germany and Japan, Iceland and Fiji, Australia and Brunei. At this particular time, though, probably 90 per cent of the prospective customers didn't believe we would actually deliver. But there was nothing to lose. They went along for the ride, so to speak.

But it so happened that Ferranti's Computer Systems Division had just opened a super new factory, and they had no work for it. There was 120 000 square feet of brand new factory floor, awaiting a defence contract that never materialised. It was the right place at the right time. And we persisted.

It was arranged that all the letters of credit should go to Ferranti. So a large company, as purchaser, was dealing with large company, as supplier. It made it respectable. We were acting as a kind of agent, but we priced the machine and owned the rights on it. It sounds simple now, but it was enormously complex to manoeuvre.

Soon the money involved became huge. Once the figures got into the eight figures, my father decided he had better come in and have a look. Meanwhile, Ferranti took on the management of the thing, leaving us to do the marketing. They make and ship. We have the product to show. In fact, we invited all our distributors overseas to Ferranti. Not the Fijians, selling 10 machines a year, but the major distributors. Once they were over here, we asked for the letters of credit. We have since leant on Ferranti heavily, and they are delighted. *It is the first Ferranti product in a retail shop for 30 years. When W.H. Smith now use the Ferranti name, they do it with tremendous pride. Each party is proud to be associated with this successful enterprise* and, thereby, with us. I now get wheeled in to see Ferranti's chairman and chief executive. They realised that marketing was their missing element, and we had it, with flair.

We're now just seven of us here. Four of us in management. All family. I financed the whole development myself, raising a couple of million by extreme fleet footedness. The venture capitalists asked for an unbelievable stake, so I discarded them. Sales have built up from our original distributors to tens of millions in no more than a year. But that still left the UK market. We went straight to the top. We had built up our production, by Christmas, to a pretty significant level. Then we invited Smiths in. They have stated their intention to be the largest computer retailer, and we believed them.

But before we called them in, we approached the huge National Semiconductor Company. Computers break down and we didn't want to be lumbered with the repairs. I learnt my lesson from watches. It's no fun. So we came to a deal with National Advanced Systems, part of National Semiconductor. They would offer a one year warranty, in exchange for the prospect of future maintenance business, in the following years. In fact, I have a mind to write to the Chairman of Burroughs. A while back I had one of their machines and it broke down regularly. That pushed me into making my own computer, and making it well. We could have gone to Taiwan, but we chose not to. Ferranti don't make junk.

Because of the volume of business, National Semiconductor gave us a good price for doing the repairs on site. So the product is being made and serviced by first class people. W.H. Smith could not fail to have been interested. Their market development manager was extremely impressed, especially after coming to Ferranti. He shook hands on the deal there and then. Inquiries at Smiths are now staggering. One customer has asked for 700 of the machines! We're now delivering three shipments in one.

So we have a superb distributor network round the world, tremendous financing ability via Ferranti, and our own profits. If I could do all this on £500 start-up capital, what can I now do with all the profits coming in! Let's review the situation. We have a turnover in the tens of millions. We have a service organisation second to none. We have retail outlets all over the world. We are fleet of foot. While others bury their profits in overheads, we develop new products, for businesses, at different price brackets. I'm interested in the middle sector. Not the bottom, not the top.

I still live with father at home. *Money is of no interest to me. It's the beauty of having done it at twenty eight, having attained a height reached by few.* To do it and remain so small delights me. I'd loathe to be part of something big. *I can pick up the 'phone now, speak to anyone in Ferranti or National Semiconductor, and get attention.*

I'm quite happy now to develop new products without being lumbered and encumbered. We have more orders than production. *I can decide who gets what.* In five years we shall be a huge company, and at the same time very small. We are looking to integrate backwards, while still keeping no more than seven people. By then we will have a brand name, respectable in our own right.

We want to be the people who put a computer on everyone's desk, while retaining a low profile, and keeping in the background.

****
Acquiring resources
****

– as **risk taker,** taking chances

the entrepreneur is a proverbial risk taker

– as an **opportunist,** spotting chances

he sees opportunities, where others see problems

– as a **wheeler dealer,** making chances

the entrepreneur negotiates with his environment to benefit himself

– as an **achiever,** he secures results

for the entrepreneur it is results that, in the end, always count

– being **powerful,** he is able to influence people

securing power is part and parcel of his way of being

– as a **product champion,** he commits himself

the entrepreneur within a company is often a 'product champion'

– as a **marginal man,** he secures an edge

within the company or without, he is a 'marginal man'

– as a **modern gamesman,** he enjoys himself

the modern entrepreneur is less of a 'jungle fighter', more of a 'fun lover'

risk-taker – I take chances

- You believe that the future will turn out in your favour
- You enjoy taking calculated risks

opportunist – I spot chances

- You see the creation of customers as fundamental to your business
- You expand outwards, like an amoeba, and then fill in the spaces

wheeler dealer – I make chances

- You put together a system of exchange and transaction by doing deals
- You combine ideas, skills, money, facilities and markets into a profitable combination

achiever – I secure results

- You bring your desirable future into being
- You are a persistent problem solver, patient, determined, competitive

powerful – I influence people

- You seek, defend, and increase your power
- You get into a position where you can dictate the moves

champion – I commit myself

- You identify with an idea, as your own, and vehemently promote its cause
- You combine your desire for independent action with a commitment to the organisation

marginal – I establish an edge

- You are marginal to the social order
- You are obliged to find a niche rather than to fill a role

gamesman – I enjoy business

- You control your environment
- You respond to work and life as a game

****

John Harvey Jones is a charismatic leader who, in the short space of three years, has managed to transform the ICI Board. Its function has shifted significantly from individual to collective responsibility, and from functional strategy to business regeneration. But while creating new enterprises has become a major concern of ICI, it is not management's responsibility to set up individual concerns. Such business creation is the function of the entrepreneur.

THE NEW ENTREPRENEUR

Jack Dangoor, of Advance Technology, is a new entrepreneur, who has created a business from scratch. In a couple of years Dangoor's business has grown from almost nothing to tens of millions of pounds. But the approach he has taken is not that of the go it alone 'self-made man', but of the coalition builder who has established strong alliances with the establishment. In that sense he is a new entrepreneur – more of a 'gamesman'[1] than a 'jungle-fighter'.

THE ENTREPRENEUR IN HISTORY

Whereas our recent preoccupation has been with managers, the originators of business were of course entrepreneurs. Prior to the Industrial Revolution, commercial traders bought in one country, sold in another, and some built up trading empires. Not surprisingly, classical economic theory located the entrepreneur at the centre of its micro economy. He was the risk taker; he assembled together the land, labour and capital, and he was motivated to maximise profits and to create wealth.

In fact, the word 'entrepreneur' pre-dates economic theory, and is derived from the French. It originally represented the 'active person', who gets things done in any walk of life. Sixteenth century French writers referred to Trojan warriors as 'entrepreneurs' hardy and usurping, intent on risking their lives and fortunes. Other French writers and philosophers linked entrepreneurship with the art of cultivation. It was only in the seventeenth century that the term began to be applied most particularly, in an economic context.

A RISK-TAKER, taking chances

The classical economists of the nineteenth century did the entrepreneur both a service and a disservice. On the one hand, they brought him onto centre stage, as the originator and orchestrator of enterprise. Yet, on the other hand, they rendered him impersonal and characterless. So while he was certainly in the spotlight, a shadow seemed to be cast over his actual shape and features. That shadow has remained, particularly in Great Britain, until only recently.

There are remarkably few books of any worth written about entrepreneurs. Whereas the management literature abounds, that on entrepreneurship is extraordinarily scarce. The only nineteenth century economist to provide us with any real insight into the entrepreneur was the Austrian political economist, Joseph Schumpeter. In his *Theory of Economic Development* he portrayed entrepreneurship as a positive and disruptive force, keeping everyone on his toes, and constantly breaking up the old order by introducing new ideas and products. Schumpeter would have welcomed Jack Dangoor coming in with his 'Advance Technology', at a fraction of the cost of IBM's personal computer – positively disrupting the establishment.

> ... the social function of the entrepreneur is not only to introduce something new into economic development, to invent, to discover, and to diversify products, but also to spread new methods of organisation and manufacture, and to adopt and popularize the inventions of others. He does not confine himself to the efficient management of the existing economic system according to traditional rules, but at each moment, by his initiative and bold faith in the future, he threatens the habits of customers and therefore the sources of profit of his more conservative competitors.[2]

Schumpeter was writing in the early part of this century, and it was not until the 1960s that another serious work on entrepreneurship appeared. A group of Michigan University sociologists, Collins, Moore and Unwalla, wrote a book *Enterprising Man*, based on interviews with some 200 local small businessmen:

The term entrepreneur evokes various images. In the popular conception, a risk taker, a man who braves uncertainty, strikes out on his own, and through native wit, devotion to duty, and singleness of purpose, somehow creates business and industrial activity where none existed before. At the same time, the term engenders certain negative overtones. There is a connotation of manipulation, greed and avarice, and grasping acquisitivenesss. While it is true that the entrepreneurial hero built railroads and canals, there is also the implication, that, in the process, he befouled nature, and generally ravaged the rational order of things.[3]

This ambivalence has plagued our minds, to the extent that, for at least thirty years in this country, the entrepreneur was completely out of popular favour.

In America, the small businessman has always remained a popular figure, but, like in Britain, entrepreneurship has been banished from most of the corridors of corporate power. It has only been in the last few years, particularly since E.F. Schumacher published *Small is Beautiful,* that the idea of an 'enterprising organisation' has regained its popularity. Schumacher was a German, who emigrated to Great Britain, and became the great philosophical supporter of small business.

An OPPORTUNIST, spotting chances

Few people know that Schumacher placed at least as much emphasis on achieving smallness within large organisations, as upon smallness per se. Although big companies have not been a traditional stamping ground for entrepreneurs, the situation is changing. It is also very noticeable that Jack Dangoor set up his vital connections with entrepreneurial managers within three big companies, Ferranti, W.H. Smith, and National Semiconductors. He has been not only a 'positive disruptor' but also a 'positive connector'. Jack used the big organisations to gain leverage for himself. They used him to 'import' product (W.H. Smith) and market (Ferranti) awareness. Both John Rowland, at W.H. Smith, and Tom Bithall, at Ferranti, were therefore opportunistic in their own way.

They have acted as the 'entrepreneurial managers' that the American, Charles Dailey, describes in a book of that name. In comparing the 'languages' of the 'entrepreneurial', as opposed to the conventional, manager, Dailey maintains that:

> The entrepreneur speaks a language which enables him to compare the Ought and the Is, because his role is to bring the desirable future into being. This, in turn, requires him to speak a language which refers to the environment as well as to the organisation. Only environmental response can tell him what is desirable in relation to sales, votes, cures . . .[4]

And it is in the environment that the opportunist spots his chances, and does his deals.

A WHEELER DEALER, making chances

Entrepreneur and manager fit like hand in glove within any successful business organisation. Whereas entrepreneurial activity pushes out, managerial activity draws in. Whereas entrepreneurs make chances, by putting deals together, managers minimise the chances of the deals going sour. Jack Dangoor put a terrific deal together only because he had the courage and insight to make real space for himself. He gave chance a chance. He took a chance. He grasped his chance.

The differences between your archetypal manager, and entrepreneur, are set out schematically below:

'Entrepreneur'	'Manager'
Achieving results	Objective setting
Risk-taking	Policy formulation
Tactical planning	Strategic planning
Negotiating	Organising
Inter-personal communications	Formal communication
Trouble shooting	Control

The entrepreneur is very much a negotiator, and a trouble shooter, rather than a planner and an organiser. As our American sociologists found, in their study of Enterprising Man:

> The business hierarch climbed to success in an established social and authority structure. His tools were occupational proficiency and social skill. He rose because he had a positive attitude toward authority. Having arrived, he perceives his role as one of social leadership in an established organisation . . . The enterprising man . . . built his own structure . . . not hierarchical and bureaucratic, but rather a system of exchange and transaction, one that he put together by making deals. He does not perceive his role as one of leadership so much as one of being a key figure in a transactional system.[3]

Jack Dangoor learnt how to negotiate in the watch market. Now, in the computer business, he has become a key figure in a transactional system, doing deals with customers, distributors and suppliers, exchanging insight and fleet footedness for credibility and know how.

AN ACHIEVER, securing results

It is not money that motivates Jack. He wants to be the person who put a computer on everyone's desk. His great achievement is to have attained a height reached by so few, by the age of twenty eight. As a good negotiator, a wheeler dealer, and an entrepreneur, he is motivated by achievement.

David McLelland, the American psychologist who has spent many years studying the need for achievement in different cultures, has come to the following conclusions. The achievement oriented person is attracted to tasks that involve skill. Unlike the gambler, he prefers moderate risks, and he tends to be realistic. He likes to do a job well, for its own sake, and he plans and directs his energies accordingly. He is a persistent problem solver, and obstacle remover, patient, determined and competitive. When there is a job to do that needs help, he draws on experts. He has a lesser need for closure, and for black and white solutions, than he who is not achievement oriented. He has good, practical intelligence, is able to think clearly under stress, has good product knowledge, and an ability to perceive and exploit power.

Being POWERFUL, influencing people

Power is something dear to the hearts of both entrepreneur and entrepreneurial manager, though it is not a subject that the management literature copes with particularly well. The exception to this rule is Michael Korda, himself a publisher and businessman, who has written an intriguing little book on power in organisations. From the outset, he claims that the trick is to develop a style of power based on one's own character and desires. He also maintains that it is better to set things up quietly, and behind the scenes, rather than cause friction up front. Power is not static, but must be sought, defended, increased and protected by cleverness and originality. It is neither good nor bad in itself, but it all depends how it is used, and to what end.

The most useful part of Korda's book, for our purposes, is the part that distinguishes the 'expander', from the 'ladderer'. The latter, representing the orthodox manager, is promoted in the normal way, one step at a time. He rises up the formal hierarchy, within a single company, or from one to another. In the first case it is continuous, and, in the second, discontinuous, but in both cases it is predictable. The 'expander' is different:

> ... instead of moving upward, he expands outward, flowing like lava, gradually enveloping enough people and functions, so that they have to be promoted to regularise their acquisitions. These are made, as it were, by reaching out arms like an amoeba, and then filling in the spaces. Even when they have acquired the power they seek, they are careful not to establish a fixed hierarchy to replace the one they have destroyed. You can't knock them off their perch because they have none! The moment somebody begins to spread out like a tide, it floats away.[5]

Advance Technology has expanded dramatically, in just such a way. Remember that Jack wants to achieve great things, but, at the same time, to retain a low profile, and to keep in the background. He now commands the power to pick up the phone and get through to the 'top brass' in Ferranti's or in W.H. Smith's, but he remains unencumbered by prestigious offices. He operates from the back streets of North London, with seven people, while he controls millions of pounds. Jack is a bit like 'Vaci', a project manager I know in ICI Paints, who commands tremendous authority in the organisation, and works from a tiny office, with no secretary. He is a product champion, and not part of the formal organisation structure.

As product CHAMPION, committing himself

In the 1970s a spate of 'New Ventures' departments were created, in large American corporations, to stimulate new business activities. The organisational changes were only moderately successful, and by the 1980s, most of the departments had disappeared. One of the main reasons for their demise, was the lack of so-called internal entrepreneurs to champion the new products. Much of the literature on new venturing comes to the conclusion that it is the 'venturesomeness' of the people that counts in the end. For example, Tait Elder, who in 1980 was head of New Ventures at '3M' – probably the most successful of all new venturing companies – proclaimed:

> All the activity and apparent confusion you might observe in our organisation revolves around fired up 'champions' – making sure that the champion comes forward, grows and flourishes, and even indulges in a little madness![6]

Unlike the independent entrepreneur, the product champion will not risk his own money. As a corollary to that, at least in the normal course of events, whereas he must have a desire for independent action, he needs to be committed towards the organisation. Interestingly enough, John Rowlands and Tom Bithall, merchandising manager at W.H. Smith and sales manager at Ferranti, have become product champions for the Advance computer in their respective organisations. Jack Dangoor, meanwhile, remains the independent entrepreneur, the marginal man, both socially and commercially. He took a financial risk and they took a more personal one. Now they operate as an entrepreneurial team.

As MARGINAL MAN, securing an edge

Jack has secured an edge, in the small business computer business, by remaining on the margins of the establishment, while taking due advantage of it. As an Iraqi Jew he is also a marginal man in the psychological sense, never securely ensconced within the indigenous society.

It is certainly well known that the Ugandan Asians, the Jews worldwide, and the Chinese in Hong Kong and Singapore, are entrepreneurial people, with a 'marginal' position in society.*

Seemingly, it requires insecure roots to grow entrepreneurial branches. The story of 'Enterprising Man' is:

> ... the story of a crisis avoided socially, but retained emotionally as part of his character formation ... A business enterprise is a system of exchange and transaction that has no end in any linear sense. Accordingly, the lack of problem resolution among entrepreneurs may fit their world. Perceiving the world in terms of 'irreconcilable dichotomies', may be a very realistic assessment of the negotiational, transactional environment in which they live.[3]

So it is the lack of resolution which obliges the entrepreneur to seek resolution, personally and economically. The desire to create a new enterprise emerges out of his psychological urge to create a more satisfactory world than the one he inherited. What the Dangoors inherited was insecurity and persecution. What they desire to create is an enduring, but flexible enterprise, which draws on the establishment, but is not tied to it. On the other side of insecurity is fleet footedness; on the other side of persecution lies survival.

MANAGEMENT AND MACHIAVELLI

In 1970, the controversial Antony Jay, whose career has spanned business and government, the media and the diplomatic service, wrote his book *Management and Machiavelli*. The book gained some popularity, as well as notoriety. But few people have appreciated its significance, in carrying many entrepreneurial traits and traditions into corporate life.

Jay has a reputation, in his life and his writings, for both ingenuity and self-centredness. It is this combination of traits which characterises the 'Machiavellian' manager:

> The real pleasure of power is the pleasure of freedom, and it goes back to one of man's most primitive needs, the need to control his environment. You get no great sense of freedom if you are liable at any time to starve or freeze, or be devoured by wolves, or speared by a neighbouring tribe. So you set about securing a supply of food, shelter, warmth and defensive weapons. Gradually you increase control, and one of the most important ways you increase it is by organisation, by making your tribe the biggest and strongest in the area. Your life is still regulated by the actions and decisions of others, but now a part of it is regulated by your own choice and your own decisions.[7]

This mixture of pleasurable freedom with control over others, results in an acquisitive driving force. It forms the basis for aggressive salesmanship and assertive self interest.

Jay was very much of the opinion that organisations, and their management, should be understood as an objective phenomenon, rather than as an idealised form. It was important, not to look for proof that industry is honourable or dishonourable, but only for patterns of success or failure, growth or decay, strife or harmony, and for the forces that produce them. He made use of analogies from politics and warfare and from games of conflict. Like warfare, he saw commerce in terms of the securing of territory (market share) with swords or muskets (samples or specifications). Where nations, he said, have had to graduate from bombers to missiles, just because the enemy had them, so electronic manufacturers have had to graduate from valves to transistors to chips. Many of the heads of the new electronics companies, particularly in America, conform to Jay's image. Jack Dangoor, on the other hand, is less of a Machiavellian, and more of a modern 'Gamesman'.

Modern GAMESMAN

Robert Townsend who in the 1970s wrote the best-seller *Up the Organisation,* claimed: 'If you're not in business for fun or profits, what the hell are you doing here.' As President of Avis (who try harder) he was well entitled to his opinion. In fact he sub-titled his book: 'How to stop the corporation from stifling people and strangling profits.'

The theme of fun, along with profit, was later extolled in Michael Maccoby's *The Gamesman*. In this book, based on in depth interviews with American senior managers, the author compares and contrasts the old 'jungle fighter' with the new 'gamesman'. Both are entrepreneurs, of a kind, but the one is of the old school, and the other of the new:

> The jungle fighter's goal is power. He experiences life and work as a jungle (not a game), where it is eat or be eaten, and the winners destroy the losers.

whereas:

> The gamesman is the new man. His main interest is in challenge, competitive activity where he can prove himself a winner . . . He likes to take risks and to motivate others to push themselves beyond their normal pace. He responds to work and life as a game. The contest hypes him up and he communicates his enthusiasm thus energizing others. He enjoys new ideas, new techniques, fresh approaches and short cuts. His talk and his thinking are tense, dynamic, sometimes playful and come in quick flashes. His main goal in life is to be a winner . . . [8]

That sounds more like Jack Dangoor – who wants to put a computer on everyone's desk while retaining a low profile – than does the Machiavellian 'jungle fighter'. I shall always remember Jack with a smile on his face rather than a scowl, with a twinkle in his eye and not a fierce look.

Conclusion

In conclusion, the entrepreneur is a risk taker who, like Jack Dangoor, will go out on a limb and take his chances. From the unique angle that he adopts, on business and on life, he will spot the opportunities that the more blinkered manager might miss. For who would have thought that W.H. Smith, Ferranti and National Semiconductor could have joined forces, under Advance's own umbrella, combining ideas, skills, money, and facilities, and doing it in a way that only he knew. Jack expanded outwards, like an amoeba, and then filled in the spaces. He made his approaches, and his connections, before he was able to deliver the goods. But Jack's determination to succeed, to prove himself, to bring his desirable future into being, carried him through.

Entrepreneurs, like Jack, seek to gain power and influence, not for its own sake, but to realise an ambition. They gain renown while remaining largely unknown. Jack has got himself into a position where he can dictate the moves, but he has no official status. His commitment to himself, and to his product, is only matched by his commitment to the customer and to his institutional allies. But he is not bound by any organisation. He has retained his marginal status, socially and economically. Jack's drive for recognition is channelled indirectly rather than directly. He gains credibility, through Ferranti and W.H. Smith, while he remains in the back streets of London.

In many ways, it is all a game, and Jack has played to win. In so far as his company remains small, he remains free, but insecure. Yet it is this very insecurity that drives him on to bigger things. Therein lies the entrepreneurial paradox.

Notes and references

1   See Michael Maccoby's book *The Gamesman,* for more information on the difference.
2   Schumpeter, J., *The Theory of Economic Development,* Oxford University Press, 1971.
3   Collins, O., Moore, D. and Unwalla, D., *The Enterprising Man,* Michigan State University, 1964.
4   Dailey, C., *Entrepreneurial Management,* A.M.A., 1971.
5   Korda, M., *Power,* Coronet Books, Sevenoaks, 1978.
6   Tait Elder, Head of New Ventures, '3M', quoted in Peters, T. and Waterman, R., *In Search of Excellence,* Harper and Row, London, 1982.
7   Jay, A., *Management and Machiavelli,* Penguin Books, Harmondsworth, 1970.
8   Maccoby, M., *The Gamesman,* Simon and Schuster, New York, 1976.

Planning for change – Steve Shirley, change agent

7

> I've been determined to prove a point. I wanted to
> liberate a few hundred women from some of the con-
> straints of motherhood, and I want to control my own
> destiny. I'm fascinated with the science of computing,
> and I take pleasure in business.
>
> Steve Shirley, Founder, F International

I reckon somewhere I'm the classic outsider. I used to be
way out as a child and suppose I am that way again now.
In between childhood and maturity I became a conformist!

My life began in 1933 in Dortmund, West Germany. In
1939, when I was five years old, my family was scattered
by the Nazis to the four winds. I was brought over to England
by a Quaker family, and have had a very close relationship
with my foster father ever since. 'Uncle' visits us every week.
Family is terribly important. My husband and I made a vow,
till death do us part ...

I progressed from village to grammar school, via a Roman
Catholic Convent, and loathed all three. I would have liked
to go to university, but the family could not afford it. At
school I loved maths and literature. I was fascinated by language and European culture.

Although Uncle brought me up beautifully, he and Auntie
were terrible social snobs. They took me out of the village
school because I was developing a 'Brummie' accent. I
attended some of the Nuremberg trials.

My passions at eighteen were different from those of other children my age. I campaigned for homosexual law reform, lobbied for changes in the law on suicide, and campaigned for birth control. I was very extreme. These things were so important to me. I believe in doing as you would be done by, in all walks of life.

You see, the difference between me and most other people is that I cannot keep things in watertight compartments. I'm a funny mixture. I'm a generalist and yet I have one or two all consuming passions. I came to this country as a refugee, and yet I'm more English than the English. I am happy, and yet divinely discontented.

While I was campaigning for this and that I went to London, at eighteen, to look for a job. Ironically I was offered two, and took the one with the Post Office research station because it offered better job security. Whereas some people saw me as a revolutionary, I can see myself, with hindsight, as having been careful and risk averse. I was also attracted by the opportunities offered by the Post Office for furthering my education. Four years later, with the help of its day release facilities, I obtained my B.Sc. in maths.

I loved the beauty of maths, as I do classical music. The aesthetics of form are a whole world in itself. But I wasn't clever enough to become an original mathematician. My husband is a physicist. I thought he may have wanted to become an academic.

At evening classes, I came across computers for the first time. They really were primitive in the fifties. I was still working with mechanical calculators, albeit to investigate complex phenomena. There was something very special in the atmosphere at Dollis Hill where the research station was based. There was an aura of intellectual self-confidence and scientific boldness. I had three bosses in eight years; the last, T.H. Flowers, had been at Bletchley Park, scene of the dramatic cracking of Germany's 'Enigma' code during World War II.

If only we were prepared to apply such prolonged and intense intellectual effort in times of peace as well as war. I've been involved in establishing a 'National Goal' for knowledge engineering designed to generate just that sort of focus. Themes keep occurring and recurring. The past catches up with the present, as the present reaches out to the future. Bletchley is very much on my mind nowadays, because of my preoccupation with artificial intelligence.

I am also preoccupied with Derek Shirley. We fell in love in the 1950s, when he was working at the Post Office with wave guides. We met to discuss Maxwell's equations, which to this day I do not understand! After an epic courtship (six years!) we married. I left the Post Office because I felt husband and wife need to work separately. Also, I wanted to come to grips with the world of computers.

I joined a new company called Computer Developments Ltd., jointly owned by GEC and ICL's predecessor, ICT. During my years there I helped design one of the early computers, the 1301, and I also became one of the first of a new breed of software engineers. The job was highly skilled, and well paid for those days. But my career as an employee was coming to an end.

For one thing, something in me was saying that my future did not lie in being an employee. *My era of conformity,* you might say, *was coming to an end.* For another thing, I was 29 already, and wanted to have children, preferably five. Matters were brought to a head when, at a staff meeting I made a suggestion and was told 'that has nothing to do with you, you're technical'. I was furious. 'That's it, I thought to myself, I'm off'.

I decided to go freelance, thinking I was so good that people would come knocking at my door. Nobody came for three months, until a former colleague – he was then working for Urwick Diebold, a management consultancy – gave me a break. The firm had set up a computer consultancy division, and I was asked to design the management controls for a data processing group.

By the time I finished the job I was eight and a half months pregnant. When I was asked how many people worked for me, I said 'one and a bit'. *I called 'our' business Freelance Programmers.*

When my son was born I lost interest in work for three months. That was the happiest time of our lives, for my son and I together. I was so pleased we had at least that little time. He is severely mentally handicapped, and has been hospitalised since he was thirteen years old. It wasn't practicable to have any more of my five anticipated children. Perhaps if I'd had them I would never have developed my other family, 'F' International. Life is strange.

And, if I think about it, I was originally going to be the world's greatest mathematician. I was lucky in knowing what career I wanted at eighteen. That was not to be. Then I was going to raise five children. That was not to be. And here I am. Being myself.

In 1964 I incorporated Freelance Programmers. That was a turning point. It was like laying an official foundation stone. The operation became more credible to my customers and to myself. Business was growing into more of a stream than a trickle. I had earned the status. It was also the time when I began to build up my 'panel' of homeworkers. They were the real foundation stones, and they enabled the business to extend beyond myself. They have also become the business' reason, my reason, for being.

A *Guardian* article, in January 1964, gave our business publicity and context. Entitled 'Computer Women' it said:

> One of the fanatics is Mrs Steve Shirley. A maths graduate who considered herself merely competent at research mathematics, found in computer programming an outlet for her artistic talents – working out patterns. She describes the essential quality required in programming as 'seeing the wood for the trees'. Now *'retired', with a young baby, she has found that computer programming can be done at home,* between feeding the baby and washing nappies.

If we look at the *company policy* today, we can see how it *emerged out of that need and opportunity:*

> *to utilise, wherever practicable, the services of people with dependents who are unable to work in a conventional environment.*

As our dependents grew, so did our problems, particularly with regard to cash flow. I called in Kit Grindley, who was to become my loyal friend, colleague and ally. He was both alarmed by our cash management and also impressed by what we were doing. So he wrote out a personal cheque of £500 to tide us over our first cash crisis.

Kit was not the only person who had a major influence on my life and business. In 1965 John Stevens joined as our first project manager. He was a Liberal and a fervent advocate of employee share ownership. The prospect grew on me. By the mid sixties we had 60 panel members, and in 1966 a profit sharing scheme was set up, to be later replaced by the 'F' International Trust. Gradually, of course, I shall be handing over more and more shares until the Trust holds half. And I must find a way of including the homeworkers.

The secret of our success, over time, has been to maintain a good balance between this steadily growing panel of free-lance homeworkers and our small headquarters team. Today I occupy a back seat, but in the sixties, the central 'team' was largely myself.

I remember when we got a big job from Castrol, and I discovered, after six weeks, that very little had been achieved. I donned my 'troubleshooter' hat, left my husband to look after the baby, and sat on the contract, working sixteen and twenty hours a day. I had to learn Fortran virtually from scratch, but in one week, and two weekends, the job was working. I was exhausted!

In fact, until the early seventies, when we were building up our clientele, we struggled quite desperately to keep our heads above water. I remember the time when I needed £1600 so badly, I was compelled to take out a second mort-gage on our home. That was a decision Derek and I had to make together. It was clear by then that our son was badly handicapped, and the prospect of moving back to furnished digs was not exactly appealing. But we felt we had to take the risk. The whole of me was at stake.

In the late sixties I realised I needed someone to share the burden of the company with, not just my husband or a friend, but someone with the commitment and commercial acumen to share the load. I found such a person within my panel, and we set up a dual management system. That's when the recession hit. Hardly a month would go by without news of the liquidation of a former client. And *in the middle of all this my partner left and took a precious chunk of business from me.* That experience scarred me for life, but it's where I got my toughness from. When I had originally started out in business most people I knew thought I was too soft. But, by now, *I had found out what hard times were like and I realised how much I cared. These two factors together toughened me considerably.*

After all, there was much more at stake than the survival of a smallish company. A completely new way of organising work, would be discredited. I had tapped a rich vein of national talent (I am a very patriotic person) and nobody was going to stop the flow. In fact, after making a loss of almost £4000 in 1971/1972, by the next year we were back in profit, despite a substantially reduced turnover.

It was also in the early seventies that the idea of going international first came to us. I had already altered the structure of FPL, to accommodate one of my colleagues, and renamed it 'F' (for flexible) International. We had one or two European customers, but it was our Chairman at the time, Frank Knight, who suggested we establish an overseas operation. The idea was that *the company spread its employment philosophy, as well as its computing service,* elsewhere. By then we were offering a comprehensive range of data processing services. They included consulting, hardware and software evaluation, business and systems analysis, software development and computer installation support.

Because of Frank Knight's contacts, and the high proportion of Danish women in the data processing industry, *we opened up first in Denmark.* The new venture, set up originally as a largely autonomous operation, *worked well at first and then ran into trouble. The local manager began to paddle his own canoe, and proved increasingly difficult to administer and control. We'd got things out of balance. Today, Denmark is back in profit, and subject to monthly control from Britain.*

The basic demand for our service is there in most countries. But cultural and legislative differences can make it hard to winkle out a formula for implementing our unique employment policies. They are exportable, but not in their pure, original form.

We now have operations in Holland and the USA, as well as in Denmark. I am no longer even the Chairman, nor involved with day to day operations. I see my main responsibility in establishing more and more overseas operations, and in holding the ethos of the company together. Our present turnover is 90 per cent UK based. I would like this reduced to 50 per cent over time, as we become truly international.

You know, I used to see my literary interests as a side track. Now I can see how my involvement with different cultures has become so important for our work. We have also set up regional headquarters in the UK, and have delegated project management responsibilities accordingly. Our turnover has gone up, from a few thousand in the sixties, to almost six million pounds in 1983. Alison Newell, the UK managing director, runs the UK company with the support of Jane Tozer, responsible for new business and regional line managers. One radical departure is the establishment of Systematix, to exploit the booming business systems market. The business was founded on the basis of new software systems developed by my old friend Kit Grindley.

In the meantime, I have been seduced into becoming more of a public figure. Between 1979 and 1982 I was a Vice-President of the British Computer Society. During the International Year for Disabled People, I developed several IT based projects. At the moment one great interest is the development of British excellence in the field of Artificial Intelligence. I am also preoccupied with the damaging effect that computers can have on the human spirit. Here is something I wrote for April 1984's *International Management:*

> Definitions of intelligence are often generated to suit a partisan interest. If intelligence is defined in terms of an ingredient common to several great acts of creativity in human history, two characteristics emerge: nonconformity and the vision to forge two previously alien concepts into a totally new, enhancing unity.
>
> Without such characteristics, we would have no theory of relativity, our planet might still be thought the centre of the universe, and Botticelli would have painted his nymphs in the flat, representational style dictated by contemporary clergy.
>
> The faultless repetition of a computer robot is an attack on creativity by exalting conformity and by attaching extraordinary value to quantity, not excellence. The illusion of perfection

is a dangerous enchantment that makes stagnation a virtue and creativity superfluous.

In the end, of course, it's not money that motivates me. I've been determined to prove a point; I wanted to liberate a few hundred women from some of the constraints of motherhood, and I want to control my own destiny. I'm fascinated with the science of computing, and I take pleasure in business, especially entrepreneurial marketing and sales. You know, people who join our company are very struck by the particular working environment. Apparently we're incredibly honest with one another. The way we say, 'good God, I didn't know that.' Our meetings are so open. I'm in the process of developing a credo, a charter to cover the non-quantifiable aspects of our business. *You need to be able to express those absolute qualities that are so important to business and to life. The twinning of technical excellence with a recognition of employees as whole people –* writing programmes or attending their children's sports days *– is essential to our philosophy and structure.* I have always been a generalist. I hate the way life and people get divided up. As for the future, it's like the past and the present. I started the business as an outsider, with a whole new approach to employment. Now, twenty years and 700 people later, we're putting across a new, even revolutionary message to the world. In between we were conformists putting in the organisation and the systems.

****
Planning for change
****

– adopting managerial **decision making**

defining problems, interpreting, and solving them

– espousing corporate **planning** and strategy

applying logical thinking to planning the business' over-all future

– employing management by **objectives**

as a way of charting direction and motivating people

– stimulating the organisation's **development**

by creating structures of freedom and planning for change

– **renewing** processes of organisation continually

by learning how to store and release psychic energy

– **experimenting** with organisational forms

by hiving bits of the organisation off for short periods of time

decision making – how do people make decisions?

- Formulating the problem
- Constructing courses of action to solve the problem
- Evaluating and selecting a course of action

planning – how are plans formulated?

- Long range planning as decision-making writ large
- Objectives are set as a guide to whether or how to expand or diversify
- A resource conversion process is configured to optimise the attainment of objectives

objective setting – how is direction charted?

- Deriving objectives from what the business is/could be/should be
- Agreeing the objectives, launching a plan, controlling performance, and reviewing actions
- Setting and monitoring objectives for rational decision making, for personal evaluation and for personal motivation

development – how does the organisation adapt?

- Mapping out the realities of the environment and restructuring the architecture of the organisation accordingly
- Achieving a goodness of fit between the social and technical components of the organisation
- Guiding the organisation's growth and change

renewing – how does the business renew itself?

- Learning about 'psychic energy', and how to store and release it
- Assessing the external forces operating on the company, and the internal forces operating on the individual
- Creating structures of freedom that permit the expression of imagination and the pursuit of individual activity.

experimentation – how is 'adhocracy' effected?

- Providing stability, intrapreneurship and ad hoc organisation
- 'Chunking', whereby divisions experiment, succeed and fail, and find a new strategic direction
- Problem solving, adaptively, in temporary groupings, which cross-fertilise with one another

****

Jack Dangoor has secured his own independence by creating a vibrant enterprise. He has transformed an amalgam of new products, latent purchasing patterns, and small parts of large organisations, from disparate elements into an integrated business whole. Steve Shirley, the founder of a major software house, F International, has done something similar, and yet different. While she has also created a significant business – with a current turnover of £7 million – the social change she has instigated is far more important than the commercial enterprise she has formed. By enabling some 650 women to work from home Steve has effectively changed the context of work, and liberated many people from their domestic constraints. In promoting flexibility and freedom, Steve Shirley has become an archetypal change agent.

The role of 'change agent' has probably developed faster than any other intrapreneurial one, over the past twenty years. The advance of operations research in the fifties, corporate planning in the sixties, organisation development in the seventies, and communications technology in the eighties, can all be traced back to a common cause. In fact the common thread that links all these approaches, is our intellectual prowess, our capacity to think flexibly, and to plan, communicate and to solve problems.

Managerial DECISION MAKING

The seeds that have since borne so much fruit were originally planted by British scientists, called upon in 1940 to solve military problems. The success of these 'operations researchers' in those early days, in solving technical and logistical problems, led onto applications in other fields. It was in fact in one such field – computer science – that Steve Shirley began to work in the fifties.

Operations research, which has also been termed 'management science', paved the way for a generalised approach to managerial decision making and problem solving. This approach, which has appeared in all sorts of guises since, involves:

- formulating a problem: detecting that the problem exists, and then defining it accurately.
- interpreting the problem: developing an understanding of the problem. The essential facts must be put into the problem solver's mind, and their interrelationship ascertained.
- constructing courses of action: includes collecting ideas from various sources, or generating new ideas of one's own, and building all together into one or more possible courses of action.
- decision making: entails evaluating the proposed courses of action against relevant criteria, taking into account risk and uncertainty, and using judgement to select a particular course.
- implementation: involves detailed and thorough planning, and includes a specific programme of action. Also, the plan must be flexible enough to accommodate unforeseen circumstances.

This logical and sequential approach to problem solving, or to 'systems analysis', must have been very familiar to Steve Shirley and will have served her in good stead when her software house was created in 1962. At that same time long-range planning was coming into its own.

Corporate PLANNING and strategy

LONG-RANGE PLANNING

When I was at Business School in the 1960s, long-range planning was the rage. In fact, the problem solver's logical and sequential thought processes were now being applied to planning the business' overall future. Peter Drucker, at the time, argued that planning had become the 'intellectual' movement in management.[1] He added, that business was the first human institution to have the built in purpose of bringing about change, and that the planner was, by definition, industry's 'change agent'.

Interestingly enough, Steve Shirley was intent on bringing

about change, but in patterns of work rather than in business portfolios. In fact, her business plans in the sixties were merely a commercial means to a social end. As mother and career woman she was planning to change her own life, by engaging others like her, in Freelance Programming from home. While she was operating at the grass roots, corporate strategy was being adopted by management on high. Part of that strategy was to engage people like Freelance Programmers (Steve's initial company) in installing newly computerised systems.

CORPORATE STRATEGY

The doyen of long-range planning, or 'corporate strategy' as it came to be known, is Igor Ansoff, who in 1965 published his pathfinding work on Corporate Strategy. It was a superbly intellectual exposition of the process of strategic change. As Ansoff put it:

> From a decision viewpoint the overall problem of the business of the firm is to configure and direct the resource – conversion process in such a way as to optimize the attainment of objectives.[2]

In order to solve that problem, the strategist needed to be able to answer the following questions:

- what are the firm's objectives and goals?
- should the firm seek to diversify, in what areas and how vigorously?
- and how should the firm develop and exploit its present product-market position?

Such strategic problems, therefore, were concerned with the external threats and opportunities faced by a company, and with the selection of the right product-market portfolio to deal with them. What we have here is the sequential problem solving process writ large. Where Ansoff went wrong, particularly in the sixties, is that he relied too much on logic and intellect, ignoring the non-rational influences on human behaviour. Also, unlike Steve Shirley, he concentrated on the impersonal aspects of business, to the exclusion of the personal ones.

Management by OBJECTIVES

What has proved more universal and enduring than corporate strategy is 'management by objectives', or MBO as it is popularly called. The reason is that it is simpler and more versatile than Ansoff's strategic planning.

MBO, like so many other branches of management, can be traced back to Peter Drucker.[1] He was one of the first management theorists to write about the power and purpose of objectives. Objectives, he said, must derive from 'what our business is, will be, and should be.' They must be operational, that is capable of being converted into specific targets, so that they can become a basis for motivation and achievement. They must also be developed for all the key areas of business, including marketing, innovation, human organisation, productivity and profitability.

Management by objective, rather than by function, has proved particularly important in the growing number of flexible project based organisations. Steve Shirley soon recognised that women at home had to achieve a wide range of objectives, while having to be flexible in the process. Drawing on these strengths, she developed, through F International, a particularly flexible and effective structure of project management. Objectives are meticulously set, agreed by the project team, monitored closely by the project leader, and corrective actions are speedily taken when actual performances fall short of desired.

In summary, MBO in general became popular because of its combined simplicity and versatility. On the one hand, it is a very logical, step by step, approach to management. On the other, it can be a way of evaluating and motivating people. It can be both rational and behavioural. In fact MBO marks one of these watershed periods, when there emerged a parting of the ways. While the logical approach to business behaviour continued in one direction, the same approach to organisational behaviour led somewhere else. The early seventies was organisation development's hey-day.

Organisation DEVELOPMENT

Organisation development (OD) is a peculiar amalgam. In one respect, it relates to the design activity which I outlined in Chapter 4. As such, it has served as a focal point for non-rational approaches to management. Yet, in another respect, it represents the sequential logic inherent in 'planned change'. Where corporate strategy with its products and markets leaves off, organisation development, with its people and cultures, takes off. Steve Shirley was preoccupied, from the start, with organisation development. In more recent times, as F International has become a managed organisation, corporate planning has crept up alongside. The trick is to keep the two moving along in tandem.

A major problem with OD in the past, is the way it isolated itself from the mainstream of the business. This is not surprising, when we consider its origins. Warren Bennis, one of the creators of OD in America, described bureaucracy as: 'a monumental discovery for harnessing the muscle power of the Industrial Revolution', but as no longer useful.[3] What is instead required are 'structures of freedom to permit the expression of play and imagination'.

Steve Shirley's achievement has been to create just such structures of freedom, permitting both play and imagination for herself, and also a flexible lifestyle for others.

Business and organisational RENEWAL

The planning of change, in summary, requires both an assessment of the external forces operating on the company, as in corporate strategy, and of the internal forces determining the level of intensity of human energy, as in personal psychology. Business and organisation 'renewal' which I now want to turn to, requires both an internal (personal) and an external (corporate) focus. The change agent, in the eighties, needs that dual perspective, because the worlds of people and business are converging under the contemporary umbrella of corporate renewal or re-generation.

Already, twenty years ago, John Gardner who was Secre-

tary of State for Health and Welfare in the American government, published a book entitled *Self Renewal*. This is a
masterly treatise on individual and organisational renewal,
spanning both innovation and change. In Gardner's view:

> Exploration of the full range of their own potentialities is not
> something that the self renewing man, or business, leaves to
> the chances of life. It is something pursued avidly, and con-
> tinuously. Man and organisation look forward to an endless
> and unpredictable dialogue between their potentialities and the
> claims of life – not only the claims they encounter, but the
> claims they invent.[4]

For Gardner, the self renewing individual, organisation and
society, all go together. For Steve Shirley, the twinning of
technical excellence with the recognition of employees as
whole people is essential. This focus on renewal, has been
recently refined by the concept of 'organisational experimentation'.

Business and organisational EXPERIMENTATION

In their search for excellence, Peters and Waterman came
up with three organisational pillars, represented by stability,
entrepreneurship, and 'ad hoc' forms. The organisation that
renews itself has to constantly adapt to ad hoc changes.
It therefore is engaged in a continuing process of experimentation:

> Through 'chunking' a corporation encourages a high volume
> of rapid action. The organisation acts, and then learns from
> what it has done. It experiments, it makes mistakes, it finds
> unanticipated success, and a new strategic direction emerges.[5]

Chunking, for Peters and Waterman, is a kind of hiving
off, of activities, divisions, products. The two Americans have
taken the concepts of the learning organisation, the problem
solving manager, and the ever renewing business, and put
them together. They have also come up with the idea of
'simultaneous loose–tight properties', which link together fluid
organisation forms and business activity, with a tight product-
led divisional structure. In fact, the secret of F International's

success has been the coupling of flexible projects, employment contracts, and work locations, with tight recruitment policies and budgetary controls.

Conclusion

Steve Shirley started out in adult life as a social activist, before moving on to computer science and operations research. She then turned her yearning for freedom in different directions. She planned to, and succeeded in, setting up a new business, Freelance Programmers, which would free women from the cruel choice of whether to go to work or to stay at home. From an early stage, she established a panel of women, skilled in different branches of computer services, and subsequently put them together in project teams. These teams, while being built out of flexible employment structures, were tightly monitored and controlled. Freedom was combined with constraints, and flexible work patterns with tight programming of work.

As the organisation developed from Freelance Programmers into F International, so more elaborate structures and systems had to be planned and developed. Moreover, to ensure that these structures could be continually renewed, a means has had to be found of storing and releasing personal energy. In the last few years, there has been much more emphasis placed on personal and management development, and the organisation is now wrestling with the problem of how to manage innovation. Finally, the company is experimenting with new organisational forms, including a partially hived off small business division, and strongly decentralisd overseas companies.

As operational control is increasingly taken over by a Board, and managing directors, Steve remains in the wings, not even as Chairman, but only as a Director. She now provides stimulus from the side rather than the front. Her driving force is not to develop the business per se, but to extend her philosophy of freedom and flexibility into other countries, and towards men, as well as women, pursuing new lifestyles.

References

1   Drucker, P., *Management,* Pan, London, 1979.
2   Ansoff, I., *Corporate Strategy,* McGraw-Hill, Maidenhead, 1965.
3   Bennis, W.G., 'Changing Organisations', *Journal of the Institute of Applied Behavioural Science,* vol 2, no. 3.
4   Gardner, J., *Self Renewal,* Harper Colophon, New York, 1964.
5   Peters, T. and Waterman, R., *In Search of Excellence,* Harper and Row, London, 1972.

Animating people – Nelli Eichner, animateur

8

We became one family, one group of people who pulled together for the common good.

Nelli Eichner, Director, Interlingua

I am now the director of a translation company called 'Interlingua'.

In this 'short story' I shall tell you how we started, grew and prospered. 'We' means my husband, our five children and now, with the help of a few grandchildren...

I, Nelli Eichner, née Nelinka Kleinová, was born on the family farm in what is now called Czechoslovakia. We spoke Czech and German at home. Some war prisoners who were left behind and who were working on our farm in the Austro–Hungarian Empire were Italians, and some of them were Russians.

These men were lonely in a strange land. They found it hard to learn Czech. I could not really blame them. It is a language with sentences such as STRC PRST SKRS KRK!

These lonely men were only too glad to tell the stories of their homelands to little Nelinka, who loved sitting on a cosy lap and listening to stories. Gradually I started to understand the legends of old mother Russia, full of werewolves and the Italian stories about the singing mermaids of Venice. In the evening, in bed, I repeated these stories in Czech to my little sister.

Without knowing it, I had become a translator.

When our dairymaid found out that I had learned to communicate with her Russian lover, which she could not do, at least not verbally, I was frequently sent to the pub to fetch him. The mill foreman asked me to tell the Italians that they had not filled the sacks of grain right up to the top. Thus I became an interpreter at the ripe old age of four years. My parents tried to make me into a young lady (unsuccessfully, as you will note) – that's why I was sent to school in Vienna, Austria where I learned my lessons in German, while still speaking Czech at home. French and English grammar were painfully drummed into me when I was eleven years old, but I am glad to say that I actually learned to speak these languages later, at an international scout camp.

I was not a particularly brilliant scholar, but my languages were soon just a little better than my school teachers'. That's how I managed to pass exams – somehow.

I spent several holidays abroad, usually hitch-hiking, which brought me into contact with local people. I learned to communicate, at a superficial level, in other languages. Later I was able to improve on these by reading books, papers and learning local folk songs.

Hitler made it impossible for me to stay at home and continue my studies. I accepted a job in Rome for one year, then moved to France, then England. When war broke out, I was working in the Czech Embassy in Paris.

When the Germans occupied Paris, I fled again. This time with the Czech Army. I interpreted for them and for the English officers in England who were suddenly swamped with a Czech Army, a Polish Army and the Free French Army, most of whom could not say a word in English.

I was then twenty-five years old and doing well interpreting for a living. That's when I met my husband. This was the greatest stroke of luck in a very lucky life. His name is Fred. He is a chemist, a good linguist and, to me, the most wonderful man in the world.

We were married in a registry office in London during the blitz. I soon became pregnant. Our first child, Jona, was born under a shower of bombs. I had to stay at home to look after my baby, which meant living on only one salary. We were very short of money. We had to think of some way to supplement our income. My languages came in useful. They provided me with pocket money. It helped a bit. Fred was writing a text book for an Oxford publisher. I translated the stuff. It helped a bit more.

Then our second child, our son Mike, fell ill with polio. We thought that the world had come to an end. But — somehow — he lived. He survived the illness, but his lungs had collapsed. There was but one way to save him. Take him out of London, into the fresh country air — immediately!

There was no time for house hunting and, just after the war, thousands of couples were chasing after the few small, one-family houses which had not been bombed and blitzed. We were obliged to take the only house which we could get in the country. It was an eight-bedroom country house standing in large grounds full of trees and roses and lots of very fresh air. It was also full of brambles, nettles and several holes in the roof. The plumbing was leaking in twenty three places and the electric cables had rotted away. But, because of its size and bad condition, nobody else wanted it. We were able to get the lease — FREE — provided we undertook to repair the house. We did!

From the day we moved in, our little son started to recover. Also, from that day, and for the next twenty years, we were always broke! All our money and all our spare time went on building repairs. But it was well worth it. Mike is now thirty seven, an active and very clever young man and he is managing director of Interlingua.

We were buried in the depths of rural Sussex and we just had to find a way to earn more cash to live on and to repair the house.

I shall now tell you about some of the things which we tried, and which did NOT succeed, so that you don't think that Interlingua just 'happened'.

When we moved to Ashurst Wood, my husband could not continue travelling to north London. He stayed on with his firm as consultant chemist. At home he spent his time fixing the roof, the plumbing, the drains and cutting the overgrown hedges. One of our florist friends told him that the cypress hedge clippings were in demand by florists. That's how we started supplying Covent Garden flower market with greenery.

Since my husband could no longer rely on his salary, money had to be found from somewhere – in Ashurst Wood. We raised and bred chickens, ducks and geese. Meat was in short supply during the period of food rationing after the war. Our poultry prospered but – at Christmas time we had to pluck 110 hens, plus ducks and geese, draw out their innards and truss them. Another farming venture produced seventeen goats.

They gave us unrationed milk for our children and we sold the surplus in the form of home-made goats cheese. The trouble was getting up at the crack of dawn for milking. Also, we had to pacify the neighbours whenever the goats got out and ate their cabbages and roses. All these efforts brought in cash, the hard way, but never enough.

And I was pregnant once more and I could not work too hard. The third baby was our daughter Claudia, soon to be followed by the fourth baby, Marina. She must have known that mother loved her, but was much too busy to croon and coo over her for hours. She was fed, dragged about and played with by her older sisters and brother. She was the best tempered, sweetest child any mother could hope for – and she still is.

Since Claudia's arrival, the translation side of our money-making efforts had increased and prospered in a small way. We found several locally available, university-trained women who were equally tied down by their families. Together we tackled languages which I could not cope with on my own. There was enough money, at long last, for the down-payment on our first, second-hand electric typewriter, and one of the other mums did the typing work, which gave me more time to get on with translations. My husband, Fred, having a scientific turn of mind, insisted that every single translation was checked before being sent out. In this way we started to provide good, technical translations which made sense. The word got around in Crawley New Town where many new, export-minded companies had set up shop. More technical translations were sent to us – more helpers were needed, more typewriters, more dictionaries. In a small way we were in business – but still broke.

Then we received our first order for a translation of a big, fat, technical manual. We all worked like the devil, for weeks. The last few pages had to be done at night, to get the job finished and sent out, and get paid for it. The next day was a Saturday. The Circus had come to East Grinstead. Our children had looked forward to going – but ... After a night's work I was so exhausted, I fell ill. I could not take the children to the fair and to the famous circus. The children were terribly disappointed! A family council was convened over supper. The children agreed that: 'Mummy and Daddy are working too hard, we shall have to help', and help they did, from that day on.

They delivered and collected jobs, folded leaflets, learned to answer the 'phone intelligently. They painted foreign accents on finished work, and they were prepared to do the eternal fetching and carrying to and from the translators, typists, printers.

The experience of the circus set our family into a new pattern of life. 'We' became one family, one group of people who pulled together for the common good. Now, forty years later, we still do.

Our fifth child, Mark, was born at home, without fuss or trouble, between Chapters 36 and 37 of a flight simulator manual. That's probably why he turned out to be a thoroughly technical chap.

At long last Mark started school. Father and mother were able to work undisturbed for several hours every day. We turned the oldest part of the house into an office. The fact that woodworm could be heard gnawing at the timbers and death watch beetle larvae dropped out of the beams on to our typing paper, just added interest to our lives. We were very happy, we had a real office at long last. There were now a few typewriters, a Roneo, and my translating friends came to work in the office. We were a very happy group, keen and proud of our ever growing and expanding translation company. Translation jobs included flight simulators, aeroplanes, potato peeling machines, harvesters and diving gear. The office expanded into a second room and then into a third. Our clients must have been satisfied with our efforts.

That's when the construction of Concorde was being planned. The first Concorde was going to be an Anglo/French combined effort. One of our clients 'phoned: 'How would you like to translate all the specifications for us from and into French, so that designers and engineers on both sides of the Channel could understand each other, because them frogs don't speak no English!' Would we? Oh, boy! What a lovely job this was going to be. We were all delighted, but . . .

This was a Government job and we could not really supply Government departments, the British aircraft industry and sundry boffins in Parliament with invoices in triplicate under the name of 'Fred and Nelli Eichner'. The contract was to be signed on the next day. So, we all sat down to drink tea in the evening after work and we cooked up a respectable sounding name, suitable for a company with Government contracts.

The name INTERLINGUA was born, and Fred had to rush to London to register it, first thing in the morning, before we actually signed the contract.

Fred and I were now a properly constituted and registered partnership. Our little Interlingua had grown to be a reputed, but still only local company. Our children were as proud of Interlingua as we were and they were overheard bragging to their friends about 'OUR' company. Yes, they felt a part of it, having worked with us since they were babies – well, almost babies.

In our pride and boundless enthusiasm we were always working, thinking and forward planning. That's when Fred had a brainwave. Instead of fetching, carrying and delivering our translations on bicycles, why don't we INSTAL A TELEX MACHINE?

The idea was new. Telexes were still regarded as a rare and costly installation which was used only by large, well-heeled industrial companies. There was a good reason why we, little Interlingua, could not instal a telex. The reason was £50 downpayment! A quarter of a century ago the pound was still worth a pound and £50 was an awful lot of money. But we did scrape it up and gambled it all on a telex machine. It was a gamble. Would it ever pay?

The new machine, a huge noisy monster, was installed in our lounge! Yes, no other location would have been elegant enough. It stood on one side of the fireplace in front of the piano – and a new carpet was purchased in order to set it off to best advantage.

Then we all, yes ALL, including the children, learned how to use the telex machine. When we were almost sure what we were doing, I started to send out short messages to other telex subscribers, informing them that:

INTERLINGUA PROVIDE INSTANT TRANSLATIONS BY TELEX

Our very first telex translation job came from a paper mill in the Midlands. It was just a few lines, an urgent message about a pulp shipment. I translated it and typed it and sent it back to the client within minutes.

He was surprised. No, he was amazed! No, he did not believe it was possible, it could not be done! He sent another translation by telex, just to see if we could really do it again. We did! He told all his friends in the club about Interlingua. They all tried out the new service. Yes, it really WORKED! Within a couple of weeks, one of the newspapers had heard about this incredible 'Interlingua Instant Translation Service'. Yes, one could send a message in Rumanian to Sussex, via telex, and have the translation back in Scotland within the hour! The story made headlines in 42 newspapers. The Daily Mirror gave it centre page spread. Papers in many European countries picked up the story of the 'Telex in the Sussex Woods'. Enquiries came pouring in. Work as well. And money! At long last – money!

Visitors came to see us from America, from Japan, from all over Europe. They brought work and 'could Interlingua *please* accept them as subscribers'.

It was the turning point. Within months Interlingua expanded from a local company to an international company. Our house was full of offices. Our children became expert telex typists, checkers, proof-readers. We were all so proud – and oh so enthusiastic.

The large companies who were then the only telex users,

became our clients. The workload increased and became more and more varied and interesting. One day the BBC asked us to translate a film script. It was the first of many more. We were asked to translate books, film scripts, secret documents, urgent communications between heads of state. Once we translated a telex from assayers in South Africa, who informed the mine owners that . . . 'There are diamonds in the hole'. Had we been given to dishonesty, we could have made a fortune buying up their stock because we knew that it was going to go up before they did!

Once we had to carry out a very urgent translation for a chocolate manufacturer. It was finished by midnight. I apologised to our client that some of the typing mistakes were due to the fact that my little daughter had stayed up half the night to help type out the telex. No, the client was not at all cross. He sent, to my children's delight, a huge parcel full of the most delicious chocolates.

Interlingua was becoming well known and renowned. That's how an American publisher heard about us and came to see us. In his voluminous briefcase he brought the largest order which we had ever handled. Could we please translate for him the BIBLE, plus other biblical works. Each section was based on the oldest available manuscript, whether Hebrew, Syriac, Aramaic, Greek, Latin, or whatever, and had to be put into modern, understandable English.

But where, Oh where are we going to find the translators capable of doing this work? After enquiring and hob-nobbing with the heards of language faculties, churches and Bible Societies, we at long last had a few addresses of learned gentlemen who were qualified to translate from Syriac, etc. One was in Switzerland and I 'phoned him. 'Wonderful', he said 'it will be my life's work'. 'Sorry Sir' I told him, 'the publishers want the completed translation within three years'. Another learned professor lived in Scotland: 'Will you translate the Gospel according to Luke for us Professor?' 'Oh yes' stutter stutter 'I should love to undertake such a job' stutter stutter, 'but it will take me a little time . . . stutter stutter . . . 'because I am already eighty-two years old' . . . stutter stutter . . . 'and' . . . 'it will take me twenty years!'

The largest concentration of experts in semitic languages

seemed to be in Israel, the Holy Land. Where else? Fred flew to Tel-Aviv, opened an office there, found typewriters and a secretary and advertised for:

TRANSLATORS REQUIRED WITH A KNOWLEDGE OF BIBLICAL LANGUAGES PLUS GOOD ENGLISH

Then he sent me to Tel-Aviv to interview them. When I entered the office the place was black with the flowing robes of portly gentlemen — the heads of various religious bodies. As I entered, they started to get up — to leave! 'Because', they said, 'we are not dealing with a *woman*'. I started to unpack bundles of pound notes, and they sat down again. 'No', they would NOT accept my offer of tea or coffee. 'Would you like something stronger?' said I, unpacking some good whisky. The Khadi of the nearby mosque started to get up again. 'What, alcohol? It's forbidden by the prophet Mohammed!' In order not to make any further faux pas we began, at long last, to work sustained by fresh orange juice. That was 'Kosher' as well as acceptable to our Jewish, Christian, Moslem, Bahai and Druise translators.

Eventually they spoke to me — individually — but they would not communicate with each other, except when we discussed translators' fees. They were then united in bargaining for more money, and more, and more. Eventually we agreed, and with much Salaaming and Shalom-Shalom we all got down to work.

This translation was a fascinating, interesting and rewarding job. Much of it was never printed, as the version which we translated straight from the original text often varied considerably from the version which is now accepted as 'Gospel Truth'. How come? A couple of thousand years ago the biblical texts were first translated from Aramaic, Syriac and Hebrew. This translation was into Greek. The king had ordered seventy translators to provide a translation of 'the good book of the Jews' and he said: 'Let the translation be finished within 70 days — or else!' The chosen translators scribbled day and night. Nobody checked, nobody proof-read. It was what we now call a messy 'rush job'. Later this Greek text, the 'Septuaguint' was translated into Latin, because one of the Caesars said so. But, some of the stories did not quite fit into the

Roman political opinions of the day, so they were deleted, or 'adjusted'. Large chunks were dropped, because the book would have become too long and cumbersome for the scribes to copy. This Latin text was later re-translated into English, because another king wanted the common people to be able to read the good word. So, the present St. James' version is a fourth translation. And who should know better than I, that translators do tend to misunderstand, and to make mistakes!

While all this biblical work was keeping one of our departments busy, other translators were busy finding a suitable Spanish term for 'roll-over-profits', for an urgent banking job.

A manufacturer of One-Armed-Bandit fair ground machines wanted to know how to express 'WHOOSH' ... 'WHAM' ... 'GOAL' and 'WIN' in Japanese, and could we please translate 'THE FLIGHT OF THE BIG GREY GEESE' into Eskimo! This referred to the large aeroplanes which crossed Alaska, and gave the local population the jitters.

First, Interlingua had to find somebody who could speak Eskimo. Much 'phoning to various embassies provided the reply: 'Which type of Eskimo? There are three different languages . . .' 'No, we have nobody who can speak the Labrador-type Eskimo language in England!' But a translator had to be found, so the telex was used to trace one. Eventually the Trade Mission to Labrador provided a translation and then the client 'phoned: 'Please let us have type-set copy.' Crumbs! On the same day we had urgently to set a text in 'Papiamento' and print visiting cards in Iranian. No, there was no English printer who could help us. We had to help ourselves.

A printing press was purchased and type was flown in. Later, type faces were obtained from various countries all over the globe. Suitable staff were imported who could use them, speak English, and be willing to live in Sussex.

At that time, the Shah of Persia (alias Iran) decided to give a great big party for a couple of thousand heads of state, Hollywood stars, kings and other bigwigs. It was to take place amongst the splendour of the restored ruins of the ancient capital of Iran, Persepolis. Oil was gushing from Persian soil making the Shah one of the richest men on earth. His family had been sitting on the peacock throne for two thousand, five hundred years. This was to be celebrated with more pomp and circumstance than even Hollywood could dream up. Needless to say, his own country was not able to provide French truffles, pate or Dior gowns for his noble queen. Flushable toilets had to be ordered from England, as well as fans, booze, ketchup and a machine for making sliced bread. Caviar from Russia, lotus blossom from Thailand, air conditioning units from America, belly dancers from India, and so on. Several orchestras had to be engaged from Germany, fruit from Israel, silks from China and seamstresses galore to cover the Queen's train of green French velvet with thousands of pearls and ermine. The orders were usually hand written in Iranian. Interlingua had to translate a fair sheaf of these into various languages. Also specifications, quotations, replies, and operating instructions for the electric generators, the dishwashers and the flush toilets, and so on. When it was found necessary to type out and then type-set the menus for the various banquets – we had no choice. Interlingua had to set up a fully fledged Persian department, complete with in-house translators, typists, printing units and . . . dictionaries. Although we looked for them, we could not find any because Iranian/English dictionaries were just non-existent.

The family was called in to help. Eldest daughter Jona was despatched to Tehran, where she went from one university professor to the next and, after much discussion of fees, bought up their own lists of vocabulary. She is a good looking, buxom wench, well padded in the way Persian men like their women. Her stay in Teheran would make a long chapter. Shall we say, she decided to 'put it down to experience' – but when her job was completed she was jolly glad to be back home again.

Interlingua had by now gained a fair amount of experience in the art of translating and typesetting script languages. One of our sons-in-law had built up a busy Russian deparament where several translators and their supporting cast were working on Russian texts. The Persian department was running smoothly in an explosive sort of way – and now the Japanese started commercial relations with England. There were not many Japanese in England at that time and the cooks and waiters populating Japanese restaurants were not educated enough in Japanese and couldn't usually speak English. Therefore, they were useless as translators. We left our children to run Interlingua at home and we took a plane to Tokyo. An advert had previously been placed in a suitable Tokyo paper saying, short and to the point:

ENGLISH TRANSLATION COMPANY WISH TO ENGAGE ENGLISH/JAPANESE LINGUISTS TO WORK IN ENGLAND

A long queue of prospective translators had formed in the hotel lobby long before we descended for breakfast. They had all come to be interviewed for the job, smiling all over their faces, proudly handing us their diplomas and degrees certifying that the bearer had passed with honours their English language examination. They addressed us in a language of which we understood not a single word! Eventually we found out that this 'I is velly solly nobre Sil' was the English language as pronounced by the Japanese. All these applicants looked alike (to us Europeans). But we had to choose at least one of them to take back to England. Fred solved the problem. He chose the girl with the straightest legs!

Our Yukiko turned out to have been an excellent choice. Now, many years later, she is still with Interlingua, having since married our Italian translator.

With her assistance the Japanese department grew, prospered and expanded. Japanese typesetters were installed, and Letraset was especially manufactured for us. More and more translation work into and from Japanese was pouring in.

Fortunately the tidy minds and reliable work of our Japanese department took up very little management time. So, when the oil boom suddenly brought the Arabic countries into Europe as buyers, one of our family could be spared to set up the new Arabic department. Jona was the obvious choice as she had learned to handle the Iranian office, which used typewriters operating right-to-left. She also knew by now how to read the Arabic alphabet and numbers and she had learned the intricacies of setting an Arabic text. All lines MUST finish so as to be justified on both sides, even if it means that extra letters have to be inserted into the last word, such as I LOVE YOOOOOOU, or THUS SPAKE ZARATHUSTRRRRRRRRA. What she had not learned was that ten Arabic translators, however good, educated and knowledgeable they may be, each have a temper which tends to flare up at a moment's notice. It can be triggered off by a misplaced comma, an individual point of view on the Koran, or a biased view on middle-eastern politics. All our Arabic translators were very good linguists, but oh boy, taming lions must be a cushy job compared to running the Arabic office.

In the meantime the French, German, Italian, Russian and Spanish translating departments were slogging away peacefully. The canteen was serving over a hundred meals a day, and the tea-lady was heard to say:

> The Russians want their tea black, the Italians want coffee, the Germans have theirs milky and the Arabs with the mud in it. The Scandinavian department have ordered rose-hip tea. Is there anybody in this place who wants a decent British CUPPA?

That's when the enquiry came in for the British Energy Exhibition to be held in Peking. 'Two hundred data sheets and oodles of catalogues to be translated into modern (Mao) Chinese, print two-hundred-thousand copies, beautifully bound in glossy board, full colour, of course, and can we have it by June. That's when the British Energy Exhibition is about to open. Sorry about the rush, but somebody has let us down!' They did not even ask: 'How about it Interlingua, can you do it?'

Interlingua had to be cranked up and, dutifully, went into action. A family council was convened and jobs were shared out. 'Peter, you deal with the actual translators as you can read Chinese. Mike, you deal with orders and all financial matters with clients and typesetters and printers. Jona, (she had to be called back from Bangladesh where she was enjoying a much needed holiday) fly to Hong Kong immediately and take over the Chinese end of the operation.' The family firm needed help and the family united and responded. Two months later the job was done. Peter and Jona took it to

China. The adventures on their way were many and interesting enough to become another chapter.

There are, of course, many more episodes, in many languages about Interlingua. A woman's and a translator's work is never done.

I am a happy grannie now. The company is in my children's capable hands. Our conference interpreters are travelling all over the world. A solid bank of computers helps to process translation faster and better. New ideas were added to those, now old fashioned, which made Interlingua grow and expand into an international company with offices in many countries.

During one of his inspired moments, Fred bought twenty acres of beautiful Sussex countryside surrounding an elegant mansion. This is now the Interlingua head office. On the same plot of land, each of our five children have built their own house . . . Our grandchildren play in the pool. The older children come into the office to help, and leave when the job is done. These children are my greatest blessing. They fill my heart with joy and pride. Interlingua is our family business. There is no happiness like shared happiness.

****
Animating people
****

– introducing **informality** into business and organisation

the 'unprogrammed' relationships between people in organisations

– forms of **ritual**

the social glue that binds people to tradition, and to one another

– shared **values** that unite people

so enabling them to identify, deep down, with their fellows

– corporate **cultures** sharing common attributes and beliefs including identifiable social roles and meanings

– friendliness within a **community**

to which both people and technology belong

– **animation,** as a role and a function

whereby people and communities are brought to life through expressive activity

informal – we make social contact

- What kind of informal organisation have you developed?
- What technology of keeping in touch have you established?

rituals – ceremonies unite us

- Do you hold regular 'revivalist' meetings, especially for salesmen?
- What rituals exist to protect people from things they fear?

shared values – we value the same things
- What rich tapestries of anecdote, myth and fairy tale have you uncovered, reflecting shared values?
- How have you established a 'family footing' amongst your people?

culture – there are common attributes to our culture

- In what way have you shaped values, made heroes, and spelt out rites and rituals?
- Who are your 'priests', and guardians of the corporate culture?
- What precedents and allegories, from the corporate past, do your 'priests' draw on?
- Who are your heroes, and what dramas do they enact; who are your 'storytellers' and what legends have they created?

community – we feel we belong

- In what way have members of your group subordinated their needs to the whole?
- In what way has your company become like a 'mother' organisation to its 'children'?

138

animation – we keep these attributes alive

- How do you provide access to a more active and creative group life, for people?
- How do you widen the horizons and enlarge their range of experiences?

****

Steve Shirley and Nelli Eichner have much in common. Both emigrated from continental Europe in trying circumstances, both are very talented women with wideranging interests, and both attach great importance to family. But there the similarity ends. Steve is an intellectual, whose aim is to liberate women from social constraints. Computer systems and applications are just a means to that end. For Nelli, on the other hand, her love for people and for languages go hand in hand. Her life and her business are communications between one person and another, between Chinese, Arab or Swede. And what stands out, in Interlingua, is not the formal structures but the informal organisation.

Introducing INFORMALITY into business

Elton Mayo, an American sociologist in the 1940s, wrote an elegant treatise entitled *The Social Problem of an Industrial Civilization.* In doing so he became one of the forefathers of the 'Human Relations' movement. The movement developed as a reaction against the so-called 'scientific management' of the day. So Mayo set himself up in opposition to what he called 'the rabble hypothesis'. The hypothesis went like this – natural society consists of a horde of unorganised individuals; every individual acts in a manner calculated to secure his self-interest. Mayo countered this with his own view, that effective co-operation was the key to all human activity.[1]

Of course, Mayo was not saying anything new. Anthony Jay, in *Corporation Man,* reminds us of man's primitive and natural instinct to come together in small groups. In a survival situation, he says, when we have to depend utterly on one another, and to trust one another's loyalty completely, the strength of the bond formed, if the trust is upheld, gives a tremendous sense of security through fellowship:

> The experience is an emotional and not an intellectual one, and those who share it are sharing exactly the same emotional bond that united the primitive hunting band.[2]

This emotional bond is very apparent in Interlingua, not

only with the Eichner family, but also amongst the international 'tribe' of interpreters who work together in the headquarters' homely, rural environment.

Unlike Antony Jay's eclectic approach, the 'Human Relations' theorists have become rather too rational and analytical in their approach. In fact, Nelli Eichner would not understand a word of what many of their contemporary writers are saying. Gradually, as the academic establishment has taken over, Mayo's real social concerns have been converted into a rational process for analysing, and improving, the utilisation of 'human resources'. The emotional aspects that Jay refers to have been filtered out.

Forms of RITUAL

The place of ritual, for example, has been considerably underrated by all but a very few academic writers. It is only very recently, with the new interest in 'corporate cultures', that myth and ritual has become valued.

John Morris, a British anthropologist who found his way into management education, has divided business and social activity into three: drama, routine, and ritual.[3] 'Dramatic' experience and activity is novel, significant, and characterised by uncertainty. The story of Interlingua is full of all these things. In comparison, rituals provide a safer, more familiar world. Nelli's Friday night family councils, interspersed with food, wine and song, are one such ritual in her company. It has something in common with the Japanese workers' ritual morning exercises, and something else in common with the Monday morning Boardroom meeting! According to Morris, man lives by drama, remembers by ritual, and survives through routine. Whereas drama stimulates change, ritual governs interchange, and routine keeps things in order.

While the importance of myth and ritual in corporate life has only recently been highlighted, the phenomenon has been described in Britain in some depth. Antony Jay, in fact, likens certain corporate activity to religious practice. Many companies hold 'regular revivalist meetings' at which rousing hymns are sung to the glory of the corporation and its products, and salesmen are encouraged to stand up and give 'passionate personal testimony' about what they believe! Christenings (drinks to meet a new recruit), funerals (farewell dinners for retiring executives), communions (exclusive meetings for senior managers) and occasional convocations (when top men come together from all over the world) are all common practice. Salesmen, above all, need ritualistic 'revivalist meeting', and the 'religious faith' of the converted, in order to face the outside world, with all its scepticism and doubt.

The point that both John Morris and Antony Jay are making, is that we need such rituals, to protect us against forces we do not understand, or to reinforce our very humanity. It demonstrates in fact, that we still have something in common with men of all ages and lands.

SHARED VALUES, to unite people

Ten years after John Morris' work, which was inevitably ignored by most British managers and academics, Peters and Waterman heralded a new era. 'Corporate Culture', as a phenomenon of abiding interest, was born. New terms to British ears, like 'cabals', 'skunk groups', and 'hoopla', were introduced. Such words convey the flavour of American current thinking, if not its precise meaning.

In essence, Peters and Waterman have introduced four aspects of corporate culture that guide employee relationships: shared values, family atmosphere, a common language, and general informality. Most important of all are the shared values:

> Let us suppose that we were asked for one all purpose bit of advice for management, one truth that we were able to distill from the excellent companies research. We might be tempted to reply, 'Figure out your value system. Decide what your company stands for. What does your company do that gives everyone the most pride?'[4]

At Interlingua, two things bring most pride to the company. The first is the involvement of the whole Eichner family, including, at one stage, the young children, in the business.

The second is the shared love of languages, a love that is shared throughout the organisation.

Interestingly enough, Peters and Waterman found that their excellent companies all shared an 'in' language. Because languages was not their business, they had to find a replacement. For each institution, there was a particular flavour, but the different 'in' languages shared a common thread. Words and phrases like family footing, open door, rally and jubilee constantly cropped up. Especially interesting is the 'family' phenomenon. The chief executive of '3M', Lew Lehr has focused on it, strongly:

> Companies like 3M have become a sort of community centre for employees, as opposed to just a place to work. We have employee clubs, intramural sports, travel clubs and a choral group. This has happened because the community in which people live has become so mobile, it is no longer an outlet for the individual. The schools are no longer a social centre for the family. The churches have lost their drawing power as social-family centres. With the breakdown of the traditional structures, certain companies have filled the void. They have become sort of mother institutions . . .[5]

Lehr's statement is an intriguing one. In one sense it comes across as benign and progressive, in another as backward looking and regressive. For the company has displaced the natural and local community, as a social force. Nevertheless, it certainly rings true of many a successful large company, like Marks and Spencer in this country, and it does satisfy that basic human need, to belong somewhere. Interlingua, of course, is one step ahead of most of the organisations cited by Peters and Waterman, in that their family spirit, and the family of man, have been brought together through their very product. The very stuff of interpreting and translating is sharing, and exchanging, cultural values.

Corporate CULTURES of common attributes and beliefs

While *In Search of Excellence* paid a lot of attention to 'shared values' within the corporate culture, they were only one of eight sets of attributes considered. Charles Handy, on the other hand, in *The Gods of Management,* has focused primarily on 'cultures'. Handy identified four kinds of culture, each based on a Greek God:

> Zeus, the head of the Gods, is famed for his impulses and the power of his presence. Apollo, fond of rules and order is another. Athena is the protectress of problem solvers. Dionysius, for me, is the supreme individualist.[6]

In Table 8.1 below I have described his cultures, alongside those of two more American academics[7] who have written more recently on the subject:

Table 8.1
Corporate cultures

Name		Characteristics
HANDY	DEAL AND KENNEDY	
Role culture	Bet-your-company culture	Oriented towards roles, structures, rules and procedures, job descriptions
Club culture	Macho culture	Individualistic, risk taking, winning, starring, power wielding
Task culture	Process culture	Scientific, problem and project oriented, flexible and experimental in organisation
Person culture	–	Expressive, fulfilling, free, person-centred, spontaneous
–	Work hard/play hard culture	Action oriented, 'try it' and 'fix it', speedy, active

Interlingua, in fact, contains elements of all these cultures, though least so the role one. Both Nelli, her husband Fred, and now the children, have taken plenty of risks. At the same time the organisation is very flexible, and is being rapidly computerised. Nelli has worked and played hard all her life, not only in Interlingua, but also on her little farm and in the local community. Finally, although there is a strong family bond, there is substantial personal freedom. After all, Nelli hitch-hiked from Czechoslavakia to the Arctic Circle when she was only fifteen!

CULTURAL ROLES

In addition to the different types of culture, there are various cultural 'roles'. The most important ones that Deal and Kennedy have identified are the 'priest', the 'hero' and the 'story teller'.

Like churches, companies can be seen to have their 'priests'. Priests are the guardians of the corporate culture. They are the people to listen to, when the employee has a moral dilemma, or a confession to make. The priest is the 'wise old bird', someone with a seriousness even beyond his years, who can always call on precedents or allegories from the corporate past, to allay the person's fears. His formal title is irrelevant. It is his personal qualities that count. He may well preside at the ceremonies which place the corporate culture on display, and provide experiences to be remembered by all employees. In Interlingua's case, quite obviously, the priest is a 'priestess'. Nelli has all the qualities required.

. Heroes are of a different mettle. Whereas the priests preside over the corporate rituals, ceremonies and moral dilemmas, the heroes enact the dramas. Also, there is a difference between the 'born hero' − the entrepreneur or visionary who creates a company, and the 'compass hero'. While the influence of the former is all pervasive, the latter is specifically appointed to represent a shift in management philosophy. In actual fact Fred Eichner is the 'born hero' at Interlingua, rather than Nelli. For he has been the innovator and entrepreneur, who first brought in Telex, and who took the financial risks. Fred and Nelli's son, Mike − the current managing director − was brought in to introduce proper management controls, thereby becoming a 'compass hero' for Interlingua.

Finally, 'storytellers' are in a powerful position, not because of the heroic deeds they perform, but because of their art of interpretation. In effect, they can change reality. Nelli is a marvellous storyteller, who ,has re-created the company's history in her colourful, humourous, and dramatic interpretations. Many of these stories have been told, not only through the grapevine, but also in the company newsletter which she produced. Such stories as the bible translation, the birth of Interlingua, the Shah of Iran's party, all serve to keep the spirit of Interlingua alive, and also to reinforce particular features of the organisation's culture. Between them we have tales of passion – the biblical story, origination – the birth of the company, and celebration – the Shah's grand party.

The role of the ANIMATEUR

This brings me, finally, to the role of the animateur, in its historical and cultural context. Animation, as something other than cartoons, is a movement that emerged, not in business, but in community work, in the sixties and seventies. The aim was to 'animate' people in local communities via their own cultural heritage:

> Animation is everything which facilitates access to a more active and creative life for individuals and groups, and which increases capacities for communication and adjustment, and the ability to participate in community and social life.[8]

When people, according to 'community animateurs', are restricted in their choice of roles, then their personalities are stunted. They see, therefore, participation in group life – outside the nuclear family – as a sort of social vitamin. So the job of the 'so-called' animateur, is to:

- multiply occasions for group life, and to combat any tendency for the individual to isolate himself
- foster a community [corporate] consciousness, an informed social, political [and economic] awareness,

  and a readiness and ability to participate in decision
  making
- widen the horizons, enlarge the range of experience
  and raise the expectations of people.

The animateur needs, therefore, to have a deep knowledge
of the cultural network, of popular motivation, and of methods of bringing people out of themselves. He also requires
specific skills in working with groups, managing people and
situations, and in public relations. These are skills Nelli Eichner
has acquired by practising 'animation', ever since she was
a four-year-old child. For already then she entertained
prisoners of war, on her family farm, by telling them stories,
which she translated from Italian to Russian, so that they
could understand one another. She has carried on in that
vein ever since, holding parties, bringing people together,
enlarging their horizons to include not only Arabic, Russian,
or Chinese, but also computers or modems.

Conclusion

In the current business climate, as managers attempt to create
new enterprises or business re-generates old ones, 'culture'
is seen to be either a help or a hindrance. To that extent,
the role of the animateur will become increasingly important.
In listening to Nelli Eichner's story, therefore, we should position ourselves not as bemused by-standers, but as would-be
animateurs. The fact that she founded and sustained her
own business should not deter us from projecting the situation into our own. There is no reason why our production
unit or research department should not become infused with
myth and ritual, and embroidered with story and anecdote,
in a sense similar to Interlingua's. It merely takes a particular
kind of intrapreneurial character to cultivate informal relationships, and to recognise the important part played by ritual,
and by enriching traditions.

  Like Nelli Eichner, he or she has to transmit values, which
others can share, particularly ones which are intimately associated with the product or service provided. It is important

to pay attention to the corporate culture, as an end in itself, and to build up a sense of community, in the way Nelli has done. Interestingly enough, in the recently published *Winning Streak*,[9] which has documented successful companies in Britain, the family influence is the strongest common denominator to emerge.

Finally, the role of animateur needs to be developed and exemplified, if it is to take off in the corporate environment. Nelli Eichner happens to be a natural, but, in more formal management settings, such people need to be consciously sought out. Certainly Steve Shirley, whom we have already met, and Anita Roddick, whom we are about to meet, possess animateurial attributes. Perhaps they are more abundant in women than in men!

References

1 Mayo, E., *The Social Problem of an Industrial Civilization*, Routledge and Kegan Paul, London, 1949.
2 Jay, A., *Corporation Man*, Penguin Books, Harmondsworth, 1975.
3 Morris, J., 'Three Aspects of the Person in Social Life', in Ruddock (Ed.) *Six Approaches to the Person*, Routledge and Kegan Paul, London, 1976.
4 Peters, T. and Waterman, R., *In Search of Excellence*, Harper and Row, London, 1982.
5 Lew Lehr, quoted in Peters and Waterman, *In Search of Excellence*, Harper and Row, London, 1982.
6 Handy, C., *The Gods of Management*, Pan, London, 1978.
7 Deal, T. and Kennedy, A., *Corporate Cultures: the Rites and Rituals of Corporate Life*, Addison Wesley, New Jersey, 1982.
8 Simpson, J., *Cultural Democracy*, Council for Europe, Oslo, 1976.
9 Goldsmith, W. and Clutterbuck, D., *The Winning Streak*, Penguin Books, Harmondsworth, 1985.

Making things happen – Anita Roddick, adventurer

9

> All our early recipes were natural and earthy including seaweed, nettles, orchids, henna... Our shops are like a cross between a chemistry set and a toyshop. You can try anything...
>
> Anita Roddick, Director, Body Shop

I've always worked terribly hard. From the age of ten, when my father died, there was no alternative but to work for survival and that never leaves one. My parents were Italian immigrants to this country. My father had been interned, during the war, and we children were sent to a Catholic school. Being foreign set us apart.

My mother ran a restaurant café in a coastal resort in Sussex. The cafés in the fifties played the part of modern youth clubs. In fact, before he died, my father had installed the first juke box in a café in this area. I used to change the decor about to make the atmosphere in the café more pleasant. I loved playing about with the display, especially in the soda fountain bar. It was great theatre. In retrospect, this background must have done me an enormous amount of good.

After school I went on to college. I was training to be a teacher. The same showground. During the holidays I used to work at Butlins, from six in the morning to twelve at night, to earn more money. I seem to have inexhaustible energy.

At college I had this extraordinary lecturer in aesthetics. He showed us ways of presentation, of understatement and overstatement. I went on to teach history, and was lucky to have this amazingly free-thinking headmaster. He let me do anything. I created my own special classroom atmosphere evoking the subject we were covering with the music and visual art forms of the period. The kids became totally involved.

So I did well as a teacher – it's all theatre, you know, all acting – but I wanted to go to Geneva, and work for the United Nations. I had such gall in those days that I just appeared on their doorstep and got a job in the women's section of the International Labour Organisation. Having made lots of money, tax free, I decided to travel around the world, to North Africa, India, Australia, South America and Polynesia. What preoccupied me was the local women's skin. In those hot places it should have been dry and crèpy, but it was like satin. In Tahiti, for instance, it didn't take me long to work out why. Women rubbed their bodies with a lump of stuff that looked like lard. It was cocoa butter. In Morocco women were washing their gorgeous silky hair in mud. In Mexico, I saw a mother treat her child's burn by snapping off a cactus leaf and applying the slimy juice – aloes – to his skin. When I returned to England I started looking around for these natural products. I had no luck, and my interest waned.

In the meantime, in exotic Littlehampton, I had met my husband to be, Gordon, who had been an agricultural student in Scotland. We set off to start up a pineapple plantation in Australia, but decided to get married in San Francisco instead. We came back to Sussex, bought an old Victorian pile and converted it into a hotel. Our combined Scottish and Italian work ethic soon got things going. A restaurant we took on did good business too. The combination of rock music and lasagne went down well with the locals.

But we began to get tired of the hotel and restaurant business after a while. What with two children and the work till midnight, it became exhausting. Gordon decided that he wanted to ride a horse across the South American desert for a year, and I thought I'd do something with more regular hours, like open a shop. Then a whole lot of threads came together, all at once.

I'd been over to the States for a short while and noticed all over the country car repair places called 'Body Shop'. The name struck me as odd. Then I remembered, after returning from America, going into a greengrocer, a sweet shop, a department store: I could get a choice of quantity of apples, of vegetables confectionery, and so on, but not of skin lotions, or cosmetics. Wouldn't it be lovely, I thought to myself, if I could go into a place, without feeling intimidated, and get something, in whatever size I wanted, for my skin. I remembered the women in Morocco and Tahiti and the natural ingredients they used, and planned on opening our first shop.

All the success that we subsequently reaped stemmed from the same source. We had no money. I had gone to the bank bursting with enthusiasm. But the manager obviously wasn't impressed by this fresh faced young woman in jeans, carrying a baby on her back. They turned down my request for a loan. Eventually we raised £4000, but that was hardly anything. So the ideas of re-fill containers, no packaging, and subsequently franchising, arose because we had virtually no finance. Had I been given £30 000 I'd probably have sought the advice of some design and packaging consultants, and come up with the usual sort of thing. When you don't know about something you get frightened, and you listen to business advice, even if it goes against your social principles.

Anyway, I opened this first 'Body Shop' in Brighton. The name was evocative, quite risqué in the early seventies. We set up shop next to a funeral parlour and had the solicitors after us forthwith. That got into the Press and gave us some good PR. But it wasn't easy to start with. Gordon took off on his desert trip and didn't come back till his horse fell off a cliff. By then I'd opened a second shop, and people were clamouring for new shops.

I knew exactly the ingredients I wanted to develop for my range, but knew nothing about how to make them up. I tried all the big contract manufacturers and supply houses, of cosmetics, and they weren't in the slightest interested.

I went to them saying, 'I've got this wonderful idea, can I have two gallons of lotion with cocoa butter in it? Just as it is please, no packaging'. Of course they weren't interested. Packaging is where they make all their money. So I had to do it myself.

In fact the greatest buzz for me has been developing new products. But, having been rejected by the majors, I had to find someone to make them. Not knowing where else to go I looked for a herbal cosmeticist locally. I found one, in the area, willing to make what I wanted. I was over the moon. And then I came across my protégé. A young herbalist rang up after he'd heard about me. He is, like me, a committed ecologist. He's produced some incredible stuff for me over the years. It's fun. Such fun.

The timing of everything, when we started in March 1976, was perfect. Many people had become frightened by recent chemical scare stories. There was a great swing towards health foods, and people were beginning to become more concerned about the environment. The development of jojoba plant-based products, for example, was in direct response to calls to save the endangered sperm whale. All our early recipes were natural and earthy including seaweed, nettles, orchids, henna and so on. People came back again and again. Our shops are like a cross between a chemistry set and a toy shop. You can try anything, mix your own perfumes, play around and have fun.

When Gordon came back, after I had opened our second shop, we decided to go into franchising. Potential franchisees were queuing at the door. In any case, we didn't have the money to finance ourselves. To open up a shop in a prime site on the high street now will cost you £80 000. That's a huge bite into your resources. Franchising is also a fantastic motivator. In retailing the biggest problem is staff. Yet when people run their own business they discover hitherto untapped energies.

We now have 54 franchised outlets in Britain, and 56 abroad. Girls who started here as assistants, or on the stalls in Camden market, now have their own business, turning over a million pounds a year. To see it now is my pat on the back. When, in 1984, we got our placing on the Unlisted

Security Market, people expected us to feel an incredible achievement. Certainly we felt, by then, that we had made it financially. But I get my real sense of achievement out of seeing these women running their own successful businesses. It's easy for people who have the money, but a lot of our women started with as little as I did. In the old days it was very inexpensive to buy in. And even today we have a system where the bank guarantees fifty per cent of the start-up capital.

Only 7 of our 110 shops are owned by us. Our most popular locations abroad are Canada, Finland and Sweden. We produce something like 300 different products, notably hair shampoos, hair conditioners, skin creams, cleansers, oils, lotions, soaps and perfumes. We are essentially in the business of skin and hair care. Our target market is women of 18–35, but the range is expanding all the time. None of our creams is priced at more than £3.00, so we are accessible to all. I look after product development, shop design, publicity, marketing and staff, while Gordon looks after the finance and administration. Our turnover is currently running at about £5 million, with an anticipated pre-tax profit of some nearly £1 million.

As far as the cosmetics industry is concerned, we have broken just about every rule in the book. We've never marketed hope. We've never packaged. We've never advertised. We're not controlled by design groups. We're the only company who offer six sizes of one product, who refills, the only ones who offer a choice of mud, herbal and conventional shampoos.

Our herbalists will come out of the laboratories to talk to the customers and the assistants are trained on how the products are made and on their suitability for the individual's needs. I continue to develop new products via my travels to overseas countries. Wherever I go I do a lecture on cosmetics, in a hall, or in the marketplace. I then turn the talk inside out and get information from my audience. I find out about their birth and death rituals. Extraordinary folkloric information. They fill in questionnaires for me on how their mothers or grandmothers wash their hair, and that kind of thing. I look for old recipes, and then go to

Kew, or write to their university, to find out more about them. I get more detail on a particular material or crop. That way we amass an amazingly comprehensive collection of indigenous recipes. Often I get them substantiated by scientific data, because that's what some people want.

A year ago I wrote to Quaker Oats in Chicago. We use lots of oats in our products. I asked them whether they have developed cosmetic uses for oatmeal. They sent me information on Oatpro, a by-product of theirs, which can be used for eye make up. We've now converted it into liquid foundation. It spurred me on to writing to the Milk Marketing Board. There are these milk mountains, and people want milk baths. But the Board came up with nothing, so we'll have to develop a product ourselves.

Aside from developing new products, I've always enjoyed the momentum of the High Street. There's a constant coming and going. You cannot stand still. The basic house in which you accommodate your product changes. The products don't. I love that change area. There's a buzz. I also love knowing that we have unique and inidividual strengths. Who else has a perfume bar where you can try things out, and even mix your own products? I've learnt a lot about window display, and we're improving all the time. It's also important to educate your customers, in one or two sentences!

We'll always be adding new products. The problem is deciding which ones to drop. We're influenced by current developments. Our now famous peppermint foot location was produced after meeting sponsors of the London Marathon who expressed a hope that something could be formulated for bruised, sweating and aching feet! The elderflower eye gel was a direct response to pleas from girls operating computer terminals who were suffering from eye strain. But we draw a line at anything that doesn't involve skin or hair care. After all, we're so good at what we're doing, why should we go elsewhere? We're not tempted to diversify.

But we're going to open many more shops. We control them extremely well. There's going to be incredible growth in Europe. Germany is bizarre! It's absolutely biting. That's going to be a huge market. We should have 30–40 shops in Scandinavia over the next two years. Once we have 20 shops in a country we contract out the manufacturing. At the moment most of the manufacture of our products in England is also sub-contracted out.

The other thing we want to do in the near future is to establish a training school. Our sales are only as good as our girls. We're converting part of our Marlborough Road store into a training establishment, where we'll bring in lectures on merchandising and motivation, as well as top herbalists, masseurs, and make-up artists. You sell by having the knowledge. If it works we'll want to open the place up to the schools.

At the moment, we are in the process of producing for schools, an information project pack on the cosmetics industry – exploding the myths, current and historical data, employment in the industry, opening areas for class discussion, all aspects of this vibrant industry. When that pack and 'The Body Shop Book' are completed we'll really have something!

Finally there's the proposed massage school. I believe absolutely in the healing power of touch. Massage is the one way you can instantly relieve stress. They should be using it in mental institutions and hospitals.

I opened up as an alternative business. The wealthy have choice, but other people often don't. I like to think of my customers as if they were one-parent families. Those are the people we opened our shop for. Now that we have gained financial security, we want to give something back to society.

****
Making things happen
****

– **working** hard
sheer physical effort

– **acting** a part
'moving' people, physically as well as emotionally

– **physical** activity
being involved with physical products

– **health** care
exercise and nutrition

– physical **adventure**
venturing into the physical unknown

– alleviating **stress**
the art of relaxation

156

working – how hard do you work?

- How much physical effort do you put in?
- Do you have staying power?
- Is hard work part of your heritage?

acting – do you move people?

- Are you an energiser?
- Are people around you, invariably, physically active?
- Do you make a physical impact on others?

physical involvement – is your product or service physical?

- What is your tangible end product?
- Is it something people can touch and feel?
- Are you sensually involved with your physical product?

health care – how fit and healthy are you?

- Do you eat nutritionally?
- Do you exercise regularly?
- Are you bounding with energy?

adventure – how adventurous are you?

- Are you an explorer?
- Do you enjoy travelling to unknown parts?
- Do you get a thrill out of risking life and limb?

stress – how do you conquer stress?

- Do you know how to relax?
- Do you take time off to be still, to meditate, to unwind?
- Do you balance physical, mental and emotional activity?

****

Nelli Eichner has been physically active all her life. When she is not working in the business, she is working in the kitchen, in her greenhouse, in the chicken run, or with her home computer. But Nelli is of a different generation from Anita Roddick. For her, physical work is not accompanied by the exercise and health care that, for many of us today, has become a way of life.

For Anita Roddick, who created the 'Bodyshop', hard work and health care have gone hand in hand. Her business is her life, physically. She personally has developed the natural cosmetics that Bodyshops sell to the general public.

In the last few years, there has been a resurgence of interest not only in physical health in general, but also in executive stress, in particular. But because these are specialised fields outside the general managerial domain, I have not included them here. There are no end of books and articles on the subject that the reader can follow up – or will already have done – at his or her leisure.

Needless to say, the redoubtable Peters and Waterman have included a chapter entitled 'Bias for Action' in their book. In it they introduce such concepts as 'organisational fluidity', 'keeping things simple', and 'management by walk-about'. They maintain that:

> There is no more important trait among excellent companies than an action orientation ... these companies ... don't give in and create permanent committees ... don't indulge in long reports ... aren't transfixed with organisation charts or job descriptions ... Ready ... Fire ... Aim ... That's enough.[1]

But the two Americans, in talking about action, fail to consider ways in which physical energy may be maintained and developed to sustain this. That is what I want to do now, but only with reference to Anita Roddick.

WORKING hard

Anita had no alternative but to work physically hard, from childhood, to help the family survive. In that respect her situation is no different from many an immigrant entrepreneur who has had to pull him or herself up by their own bootstraps. But hard work in itself offers no guarantee that things will happen. There is more to the 'Adventurer' than that.

ACTING a part

'Acting', in the theatrical sense of the word, involves doing with a difference. Together with such acting comes the ability to 'move' other people. Such movement is both physical and emotional. In the restaurant, at Butlin's holiday camp, and now in the business, Anita has the capacity to move people to do things, in both senses of the word. She has brought together playground, show ground, and hunting ground – metaphorically speaking – under one roof.

PHYSICAL involvement

Anita's business is to provide people with bodily comfort, particularly for the skin and hair. She is physically involved with natural products of the earth, like mud which is rubbed onto people's bodies. Physical contact, in that sense, is part and parcel of her work. The fact that she is constantly in touch with such raw materials undoubtedly affects her attitude to physical things. She is used to getting her hands dirty from the 'muck' if not 'brass'. 'Manufacturing industry' comes as second nature to her.

HEALTH Care

The difference between Nelli Eichner's generation and Anita Roddick's is that the latter is much more health conscious. Whether through exercise, relaxation, nutrition, or natural skin products, the need to keep oneself physically healthy, has become a high priority for many people. Obviously Anita is one of them. She does not take the fact that she had 'inexhaustible energy' as a child, for granted. She works consciously at keeping her hair, skin and body healthy.

Physical ADVENTURE

In order to find all the natural products for her business, Anita has had to travel to the remotest parts of Africa, Asia and Latin America. Like her husband, who rode through Patagonia on a horse, she is attracted by the physical adventure involved in venturing into the unknown. Unlike the conventional entrepreneur who takes financial risks, Anita also has taken physical ones. That, for her, is part of the joy of life and business. She is a modern day business adventurer.

Active MOMENTUM

Apart from venturing into the unknown, Anita also enjoys the momentum of the High Street. Like the busy market bazaars in Zanzibar, or the streets full of people in downtown Hong Kong, Anita enjoys the buzz of constant, and visible activity. She likes the perpetual coming and going of people and products.

Alleviating STRESS

Finally, and very importantly, Anita needs to be able to relax, and to alleviate the stress caused by constant mental, emotional and physical activity. Massage is the best way she knows to achieve that effect.

Conclusion

Working and acting, physical activity and health care, adventures into the unknown and the momentum of the High Street, together with methods of alleviating stress, all serve the 'adventurer' well. They are both sources and outlets for Anita Roddick's energies. They not only reinforce her 'bias for action' but also enable Anita to remain physically active without suffering from undue stress and strain.

*   *   *

We have now completed our journey round the seven intra-preneurial types — the innovator, the 'designer', the leader, the entrepreneur, the change agent, the animateur, and the 'adventurer'. They emerge out of the seven personality types — imaginative, intuitive, authoritative, assertive, intellectual, sociable and physical. But there is more to it than that, as the final chapters will reveal. The one dimensional stereotype is no more than a starting point for our intrapreneurial journey.

Reference

1   Peters, T. and Waterman, R., *In Search of Excellence*, Harper and Row, London, 1982.

Part III

Management education and enterprise development

10

We have now had the opportunity to meet, both in theory and practice, a whole variety of 'intrapreneurs'. They come as I have outlined, in seven guises, as shown in Table 10.1 below. Each brand of intrapreneur is especially adept at a particular business function, as is also specified. A healthy business needs all these functions, and for this reason it needs all the intrapreneurs. How can we begin to develop many more of them amongst the population at large? In order to answer this question, I want first to look back at traditional management education and development. Then I can locate the way forward, in its relevant perspective.

Table 10.1
The Complete Spectrum

Intrapreneur	Personality type	Stage of Business
Innovator	Imaginative	Business vision
Designer	Intuitive	Market recognition
Leader	Authoritative	Business organisation
Entrepreneur	Wilful	Resource acquisition
Change agent	Flexible	Forward planning
Animateur	Social	Motivation/ Communication
Adventurer	Physical	Physical activity

The evolution of management development

THE AGE OF INNOCENCE

Management education and development has been through three distinct phases. Initially, until the 1950s, there was no conscious development of managers. They merely evolved, learning from experience, and rising to the top if they had the innate talent. Management, as art or science, was ill defined. Whereas, in Britain, Europe and America general, technical and professional education was well established, management education barely existed. I call this period, from say 1850–1950, the 'age of management innocence'.

THE ERA OF THE MBA

In the 1950s, the business schools were born in the UK, following the trend in America. By the time I arrived in Britain, fresh from Central Africa and North America in 1970, business and management studies were spreading to the Polytechnics. This period, from the 1950s to the 1970s, was the academic heyday, as far as business and management education was concerned. A strong belief had arisen that management could be taught in the classroom, albeit with a good dose of case studies and business games – preferably computerised. I remember studying 1000 such cases myself, at Harvard Business School, and resolving thereafter never to look at one again! I call this second era, the age of the MBA (Masters in Business Administration).

THE AGE OF ACTION LEARNING

Some time during the 1970s, the heyday of management education came to an end. Once some disenchantment with the Harvard case study method had set in, things could never be the same. A growing number of practical managers and so-called 'experientially' biased educators began to argue against the 'academic' approach. It was in this period that 'in-house' training was developed, on a significant scale. Outside of the business and management schools, emerged a growing number of independent trainers and consultants who worked directly with companies to develop tailor-made programmes. They often based their activities upon 'on the job training'. It was at this point, in the mid seventies, that the 'learning cycle' became very popular. The idea of alternating between theory and practice, action and reflection, began to appeal to many managers. Classroom based learning lost much of its appeal.

The one figure that stood out during this period was Reg Revans[1] who had deserted academia (or had it deserted him?) to plough his lone 'action learning' furrow. Revans, an Olympic long jumper and Cambridge physicist, did his early work on improving productivity in the mines and hospitals. He believed that 'comrades in adversity' had more to learn from each other, albeit in a structured learning environment, than from experts on high. They key was for the miners, nurses, or managers, to be able to alternate between action and reflection, in the company of their fellows. So he conceived of the action learning 'set', whereby a group of five or six meet at regular intervals, with a 'set adviser' or convener, to learn both from their own experiences, and also from their comrades. Having applied Revans' principles for some five years now to the development of managers and entrepreneurs, I am very much a disciple. In fact, I am inclined to call the period, from 1975–1985, the 'age of action learning'. The Business Schools have certainly not been eclipsed, but healthy rivals have developed alongside.

THE ERA OF BUSINESS DEVELOPMENT

But now, in the middle of the 1980s, I do believe we are entering a fourth era. In this one, the three previous eras will live on, and even thrive. Many of the hi-tech companies in particular have re-entered the 'age of innocence', whereby entrepreneurial managers learn by their own experience, and mistakes, to sink or swim. Conventional management education still has its place, although increasingly for students from overseas, or for UK based students on a part-time basis. The number of independent consultants is growing every day, together with action-learning based programmes of one kind or another. Yet, paradoxically, while all this is happening, the role of education and training in management is generally remaining peripheral to the mainstream of business!

This should come as no surprise. For very few people, including the best of our intrapreneurs, are aware of the potential of real education – as opposed to conventional instruction and training. The trouble is that, in the past, the most imaginative of the educational approaches have been restricted to the non-essential aspects of business. Production, marketing and finance have remained largely untouched by organisation development. It is only now, when OD is becoming supplanted by business development, that there is really potential for educationally based management change. So I am going to call this fourth era the age of business development.

Up until now, while all the conventional management training was going on, the real path to management development lay elsewhere. Judging from the many corporate intrapreneurs I have spoken to, real development for them, took place through a series of very challenging business assignments. It was their response to these very varied, often stressful but usually satisfying jobs, that proved all important. In fact, as a management educator looking back over the past fifteen years of my career, I am reminded of the man who lost his keys in the snow. Joined by a companion, he was asked why he was looking in a particular spot. He responded, 'because it's light over here'. His companion then asked, 'could you have lost it somewhere else?' He replied 'I lost it over the road, in fact, but it's too dark to see over there.'

I feel as if we have been examining and re-examining business and management education, over the years, because it has been 'too dark to look' in more significant places. Revans has made a very good start with action learning, but even that is often isolated from the mainstream of career development and business strategy. So, our fourth era is calling for an integrated approach to 'Development' that cuts across business and management, product and personnel. Developing intrapreneurs, unlike management development, must involve the interweaving of both action and learning within the business' integrated development. How, then, might this be brought about? I shall start to answer this in general, and then, in the final chapters, become particular.

The characteristics of development

THE CONTEXT OF DEVELOPMENT

The objective of management education is to develop effective managers, both as specialists – particularly in production, marketing, finance, personnel and data processing – and in general. In actual fact, it has always proved easier to educate specialists (rather than generalists) because programmable techniques are more applicable to compartmentalised situations. The objective, in developing intrapreneurs, is an entirely different one. Let me try and develop it, step by step.

First, development, unlike management, cannot be isolated from the business as a whole. The objective, therefore, is to develop the business and the people at one and the same time. Here I am saying the same things as Revans, except I substitute 'business' (my concern) for organisation (Revans' concern). The reason for focusing on business is that, like the Japanese (and, according to Peters and Waterman,[2] the best American companies) I feel that it is extremely important, and it takes a long time, to understand a particular business and industry. Interestingly enough the new, hi-tech businesses are looking for people in their recruitment drives, who understand their particular technology. This represents a reversal of a thirty-year trend that followed in the wake of the business schools, whereby an MBA was supposed to be able to manage anything and everything.

Second, development, unlike management, cannot be subjected to a single, overriding objective. Intrapreneurs seek, respectively, adventure, entertainment, flexibility, achievement, authority, potential and creative action. These intrapreneurs enable the business, in turn, to harness physical energy, share a common culture, cope with change, acquire profitable business, provide direction, fulfil personal market potential, and to create new products. There are always the two sides of the coin, the person and the business, and both need to be developed simultaneously. Moreover, it takes more than one coin to make a developing business.

Third, development cannot be fitted into the conventional organisation structure. In fact the reason that so many so-called new venture departments failed in America is because they fitted so uneasily with the organisational establishment. For a developmental programme to succeed it needs to be given equal weight so as to balance the conventional structure.

Fourth, development is a living process. Being rooted in life, and in individuality, the human personality represents its most natural starting point, even if the business represents the natural finishing post. The runner, in between, is the intrapreneur.

Conclusion: development inside out

Development is not an easily structured, or programmable activity. In that sense it is unlike conventional management. In fact, development is a living process, subject to a life cycle, evolving through crises, in stages, undergoing conscious change, while balancing poles of safety and risk, working its way, discontinuously, toward more complex levels of organisation.[3]

True development both unfolds from within and also reaches out. It is a long-term undertaking, involving several years, if not a lifetime. It spans self and organisation development (introverted) and career and business development (extroverted). It requires fluidity of movement between inner life and outside world, between self and business. So, it involves both personal and business development.

References

1 Revans, R., *Action Learning*, Blond and Briggs, London, 1980.
2 Peters, T. and Waterman, R., *In Search of Excellence*, Harper and Row, London, 1982.
3 Lievegoed, B., *The Developing Organisation*, Tavistock Publications, London, 1973.

11 How to develop intrapreneurs

In the previous chapter I dealt with management and business development in general. Now I want to propose ways of developing intrapreneurs in particular. In Chapter 12, I shall specify the kind of 'intraprise' that will be needed to accommodate them.

The entrepreneur and his enterprise dominated industry in nineteenth century Britain, as well as America. In the twentieth century managers of organisations took over. So we moved away from the personal towards the impersonal. In the twenty-first century I suspect that 'intrapreneurs' and corresponding 'intraprises' will rule the roost.

The starting point, for the intrapreneur, is neither the economy nor the organisation, but the individual. The individual is no one dimensional economic man, but a multi-faceted human being. Those 'multi-facets' are our building blocks. The successful intraprise is the one that becomes a mirror image of, or a container for, intrapreneurial variety. So it too becomes multi-faceted.

Recognising individual potential

John Harvey Jones, in an address that he gave to managers in September of 1984, claimed that the organisation must serve the individual rather than vice versa. What needs to be added is that individuals come in various guises:

The *imaginative* person is the prospective innovator. He lives in a complex, sometimes symbolic, world of his own imaginative making, and therefore seeks to set trends rather than follow them. John Dessauer, in his book on the Xerox Corporation, refers to such a character as a business revolutionary, a supreme individualist, one with a strongly personal vision to follow. Ultimately, the innovator hopes to bring about a new order of things, as a scientist, a creative designer, or even as an organisation builder. He is a unique individual who will therefore reside uncomfortably within the corporate mould. In fact he may need to be rescued from the backwoods of the laboratory or studio, so that his vision can illuminate the organisation. Terence Conran started out as a mere furniture designer and look where he is now!

The *intuitive* person is the prospective, new designer. She needs to see meaning in, and connections between, events, and is disturbed when things are not in harmony. She is likely to see meaning in coincidence and thereby believes in good fortune. She has a sense for the way things are going, and is often able to anticipate the future. She feels intuitively for the greater whole, of which each person, product or market is a part. So she can spot potential, in people or products, more easily than most. The new designer, a facilitator, understands the way people or things evolve. Her position in the organisation could range from research scientist to designer; from marketeer to training consultant. She is likely to be a go-between for either people or things.

The *authoritative* person is the prospective executive or leader. He is likely to adhere to some strong philosophical, economic, religious or scientific theory of human nature. He probably puts great emphasis on family and on tradition, both in personal and working life. He likes to make use of relevant data, and also to consult relevant authorities. He needs to work in a structured environment where people are delegated specific tasks so that efficient and effective performance is achieved. He welcomes the responsibility that management entails, in business and in the community. This is certainly the case with John Harvey Jones. Such a personality as this is likely to be found within the mainstream of management.

The *wilful* person is the potential entrepreneur, who has definite ideas about his intentions, and is emotionally attached to whatever he chooses to do. He gains a sense of accomplishment by manoeuvring people and resources and needs continuing recognition for his achievements. He believes in beating the competition before they beat him, and needs cash, property and a sense of power, for security. He cares less about the rights and wrongs of a situation and more about the reality of the power struggle. He is willing to take a personal and financial risk in order to realise significant material gain. Entrepreneurial individuals are often found in the sales force, sometimes in corporate finance, and always championing a product, if they are in research and development. They are unlikely to want to remain in staff functions and sit uncomfortably beneath a long line of management. They require freedom to manoeuvre and thrive on doing deals rather than heeding instructions. That is exactly why Jack Dangoor is where he is now.

The *flexible* person is the prospective change agent who does not want to be held to a specific identity, because of the range of her knowledge and experience. As an agent of change, she is herself changeable. She is a 'situational' person who prides herself on being able to learn and adapt. She may read a lot of books, research many different systems, or ferret around different parts of the company or environment. She enjoys being able to express her opinions and sees herself as a free and autonomous individual. She is happy to change jobs and to try out new experiences, thereby keeping constantly stimulated. She is always interested to discover, and apply, the latest trend or technique and prefers a networking mode of operation to the role of employee. Steve Shirley went a step further to create a whole organisation based on flexibility. The potential change agent is most likely to be found in a training function, in management services, in public relations or sometimes in design.

The *animated,* enthusiastic and gregarious person is the potential animateur who enjoys the pleasures of life and work, especially those requiring skill and involving other people. She is happy among a small group of close colleagues or co-workers, and relishes a family like atmosphere. She is often the 'social glue' that keeps a group happy, ensuring that there is no significant conflict. In sales, she will be the one to make the customer feel good, and, in manufacturing, she will care deeply for what is being produced. Both are very much the case with Nelli Eichner. In the personnel area, the animateur is the one that genuinely cares about others, and does not have to develop social skills. She is closely in touch with popular motivation and well integrated within the cultural network. She lives for other people.

The physically *active* person is the potential adventurer, who takes life and business in her stride! As long as she is active and sound of limb she is able to cope. She knows that, when all else fails, she can do physical work. She may pursue health and fitness, mountaineering or orienteering, movement or dance, food or wine, as a central issue in life. In one or other case she is likely to act with speed, force and intensity. She combines control − pacing herself, poise − delivering the goods under pressure, with stamina − keeping hard at it. Often we see a manual worker, who has this sort of ability, confined to activity within a very limited sphere of influence. His or her prospects as an 'adventurer' are contained by the limiting organisation structure, and restricted approach to training and development, upon which I now want to expand.

Harnessing potential

It is one thing to recognise the diversity of human beings within an organisation. It is another to harness the latent potential. Certainly not every physically active worker is a prospective 'adventurer', nor is every gregarious employee a prospective 'animateur'. In the first place one individual's innate ability is higher than the next person's. But secondly, and this is what concerns us here, potential can be much more actively and astutely enhanced than has been done before. There are four aspects to this:

RECOGNISING THE POTENTIAL IN DIVERSITY
We should recognise the dangers of categorising people too crudely. Such terms as 'manager' and 'worker' line and staff,

production and marketing, junior and senior, fail to cater for the richness of our human being. As a result we limit potential, at best, and stifle it, at worst. We have yet to invent, within business and organisation, a language to describe human functioning that is not only rich and diverse, but also parallels business functioning.

Table 11.1
Spectrum of Personality and Intrapreneurship

Personality type	Intrapreneurial type	Key attributes
Imaginative	Innovator	Original, inspired
Intuitive	New designer	Aware, enhancing
Authoritative	Leader	Responsible, purposeful
Wilful	Entrepreneur	Risk taking, achieving
Flexible	Change agent	Adaptable, expressive
Animated	Animateur	Sociable, enthusiastic
Active	Adventurer	Energetic, impactful

The spectrum of personality and intrapreneurship, as demonstrated in Table 11.1, attempts to do just that. With reference to the spectral typology, people can initially recognise themselves through a combination of self-assessment and communication with others (The questionnaire provided in the Appendix to Chapter 2 should help you identify pertinent intrapreneurial traits within yourself and others.) But more is still required. People need external reinforcement of any newly emerging identity.

REVEALING 'ARCHETYPES'

At the present time, organisations carry a very restricted range of 'archetypes' with which the aspiring manager can identify. The best known among these are the 'bureaucrat' and the 'entrepreneur'. But now that bureaucratic management has become unfashionable we are left with enterprise

alone. Admittedly the term 'manager of change' is beginning
to make a strong appearance, but it is difficult to picture
this role vividly. In fact, I see it as some 'catch all' for the
range of intrapreneurial types that I have identified.

In order to represent a full range of such archetypes, management will need to involve their 'communications' people.
This includes advertising, public relations, design, management services, and organisation development. Archetypal
intrapreneurs will need to be identified and then colourfully
represented in company newspapers, on the notice boards,
in video programmes, and in person, on training programmes.
Gradually, then, staff as a whole will begin to build up a
language and an identity with one or other of the varied
cast of characters. The object is not to typecast people,
but to provide them with a broader platform, from which
to launch themselves, than has previously been the case.
The seven 'archetypes' here can be represented picturesquely,
humorously and colourfully, respectively conjuring up images
of:

- creativity and imagination
- harmony and beauty
- law and order
- aggression and will-power
- change and flexibility
- togetherness and belonging
- energy and activity

Finally, stories can be passed on and documented describing the thoughts, feelings and actions of each.

ENTERING APPRENTICESHIP

To enable people to recognise themselves, through a combination of self-assessment and identification with others, is
only a beginning. In order to advance from recognition to
manifestation, a process of development needs to follow.

From my fifteen-years experience in management training
and business development, I have come to the conclusion
that genuine education, involving lasting personal change,
is a protracted business. There are few short cuts. As a result,
traditional notions of apprenticeship might be better suited

than our modern 'training' approach, whether academically or 'workshop' based. For the key to genuine development lies not only in prolonged endeavour but also in that blend of action and learning that results in mental, emotional and physical change.

I want to re-introduce, therefore, the terms apprentice, journeyman, and master, and also to broaden their usage. The *apprenticeship* is the seven-year period, or thereabouts, during which the individual acquires mastery of one particular mode of intrapreneurship. Once our personality changes, as should be the case with a growing human being, then we are ready to shift into a 'new gear'. The individual is not merely apprenticed to one person, but to a mode of intrapreneurship. In his twenties, for example, he or she may be apprenticed to 'adventuring' and in his thirties, to 'entre-preneurship'. Once the individual has attained 'mastery' he is in a position to move on. The person, his or her peers and superiors, will all play a part in deciding when the time has come to do so. By that time the intrapreneur will have created at least one suitable *masterpiece*. For example, a change agent might have installed a fully functioning new, computerised communications system, that suits both the business and the people involved.

In his capacity as *journeyman,* the individual will pass through distinct phases within his, say, seven-year period. These phases may or may not be marked by certification, but there should be a visible landmarks, in each case. The important point is that the path will be different for each individual, depending upon the intrapreneurial journey upon which he has embarked. In other words:

Adventurers naturally seek a path of constant MOVEMENT. They are keen to travel from place to place, seeking out physically challenging situations. Their passage will be marked by *physical landmarks,* arrivals and departures. Whereas our everyday manager will balk at the opportunity of working in Paraguay or the Lebanon, the adventurer will welcome the physical risk involved. Anita Roddick has made it her business to travel all other the world, and to expose herself to excitement and duress. Hard effort and hard knocks are taken in the adventurer's stride. Learning divorced from action has no meaning, and makes no impact.

Animateurs naturally seek out a familiar CIRCLE to which to belong. Their own development cannot be isolated from the particular groups to which they have become attached. They learn through progressive association with ever more broadly based communities. They grow through having the opportunity to create their own community rather than merely belonging to one that already exists. Each community formed, whether family, locally, or internationally based, represents a phase of the journey, an *emotional landmark* along the way. That certainly was the case with Nelli Eichner. She first established her family business, then broadened out into the local community, and then brought in a family of nations! All too often animateurs are confined to operate within a limited context, for example within a mining community, because they are not given the opportunity and encouragement to develop their social skills within the business. While the sales force and the shop floor are the natural 'hunting grounds' for animateurs, employees seldom branch out into personnel management, training or development. They therefore represent a largely untapped or inhibited resource. To harness their potential, insightful managers need continually to move such people out into fresh pastures.

The *change agents* naturally seek out a path of LEARNING. They are the most likely ones, amongst the intrapreneurs, to read management texts, to go on short courses, and to seek out varied experiences. A course, a book, or a project may serve as a *landmark* in their *intellectual* development. In fact, if change agents are not given the opportunity to stretch their minds, they will either turn in on themselves or opt out altogether. For like the adventurers, they love to be constantly on the move. But they like to be stretched mentally rather than physically. Flexible systems and modular based learning are very much up their street. Project teams, formed and re-formed, depending on the situation, are ideal vehicles for both performance and development. It is no wonder that F (for flexibility) International has developed such expertise within the company and amongst its people.

Enterpreneurs naturally seek a path of ENTERPRISE, and

one that is CIRCUITOUS rather than direct. They love to be set obstacles that need to be overcome, and to take calculated risks that are emotionally thrilling. Theirs is a life and workstyle that is dramatic, full of ups and downs, and of mistakes from which to learn. In fact they only learn and develop when given the opportunity to take initiative, to face the consequences of their actions, and to feel the impact of their decisions. The extent to which they do develop depends on the amount of exposure they have, and on the opportunity to reflect on the consequences of what happens. Action learning, which encourages people to reflect on what they have done, is ideally suited to entrepreneurs. In the absence of a formally established action learning set, they need a group of fellow entrepreneurs whom they can use as a mirror and sounding board. In their own work, they need tangible feedback and incentives, and progressively larger territories to conquer. Each battle won, each new territory acquired, each acquisition secured, is a mark of development along their *dramatic journey.*

The *leaders* naturally follow a LINEAR path of promotion, from lower to higher ends of the organisation. They rise through the hierarchy in a series of progressive steps, and accomplish their work in a similar way. They learn and develop through formal training, at Business Schools or 'in house', and welcome the opportunity to upgrade their knowledge through practically based, formally constituted courses. Certified qualifications as well as new positions with elevated responsibilities are both signposts of progress, guiding their *pre-planned journey.* Although John Harvey Jones is unlike your everyday manager or corporate leader, he too rose up the formal hierarchy both in the Navy and in ICI.

The *new designers* naturally follow a path that is neither linear nor bounded. It is lateral and ASSOCIATIVE, picking up threads along the way, and ultimately weaving them together into a distinct pattern. Because of this lateral movement they are obliged to move outside of the organisation's formal boundaries in order to grow and develop. They evolve rather than progress, and interweave rather than set a direction. So *landmarks* for them are those *significant* ideas, incidents and experiences which served to broaden their horizons

and the meaning of their life and work. Education for the
new designers has to emerge from within themselves rather
than be imposed arbitrarily from without. They need to facilitate and be facilitated, catalyse and be catalysed. Their selves
and their environments are full of potential, for development
if sensitively treated. The new designers can develop in a
rounded way if given the opportunity to extend their awareness from products to markets, or from marketplaces to
people. They need to be able to move diagonally rather
than vertically, and to integrate rather than differentiate their
experiences and actions.

The *innovators,* finally, naturally follow the TRANSCENDING
path of a SPIRAL. Over time, and like nuclear fission, their
central idea(s) spiral(s) outwards, being transformed from one
stage to another. Marks of progress for them along their
intrapreneurial journey are comprised of product/market
breakthroughs, intermingled with *flashes of inspiration.* So
Conran furniture designs was transformed into Habitat.
Habitat was transformed, in its turn into Habitat–Mothercare.
Innovators like Conran learn from imaginative leaps, back,
from whence their art or science came, and forwards, into
the social and technical future. While Conran steeped himself
in design, through the centuries, he experimented in the
world of retailing, anticipating therein future demand. His
business and his creative destiny spiralled, as he put down
progressively deeper roots. Innovators need the deepest and
firmest foundations to support the risk taking into the specula-
tive unknown. They also need the broadest scope of all
intrapreneurs, and, usually, the most wide ranging support
from all business angles. They constantly seek out fresh data,
to embellish their vision, and their learning is self-instigated.

In conclusion, each intrapreneur, on his 'seven year journey' will want to travel in a different vehicle, visit different
places, operate on a different time scale, follow a different
path, and reach different landmarks along the way. *If he
is given adequate scope* he will both acquire natural mastery,
and be ready to move on to a next stage of intrapreneurial
development.

DEVELOPING IN STAGES

There is no one path that covers an individual life or work span. We all start from different points, personality wise, and enter work at different stages, age wise. But I can make certain generalisations. The first point, which I have already made, is that if we are given the opportunity to complete one intrapreneurial apprenticeship successfully, we are ready to move onto the next. It is only when we are prevented from developing our potential that we turn in on ourselves and get stuck.

Secondly, we can also generalise about stages of development:

- Young people in their twenties are natural adventurers, change agents or animateurs, if given more than half a chance. They like to be on the move, physically, mentally or emotionally, picking up knowledge, experience or friendship along their way.
- People in their thirties, if nurtured properly, enter the age of enterprise. They want to make an impact on others, to prove themselves, to apply their experience, and to carve out a niche for themselves.
- In their forties, people begin to mellow, and choose naturally to follow a managerial or enabling path. As managers, they establish themselves in an authoritative way. As enablers or designers, they broaden out and help other people, products or markets to develop their potential.
- In their fifties some managers become leaders, some new designers broaden the significance of their efforts, and others bear the full fruits of their previous pursuits and discoveries, becoming innovators.
- In their sixties, if they have been allowed to follow a natural course of development, people enter a prolonged period of wisdom, during which they are able to review their own lives and organisations, and recreate both, thereby integrating past and present and future.

Conclusion

The stages I have outlined represent a state of perfection
to which we can aspire, but which no organisation has yet
reached. But once we have been able to internalise into
our organisational cultures the intrapreneurial archetypes, the
full variety of journeys, landmarks, and completed 'master-
pieces', we should be well on the way. There is, however,
one fundamental stumbling block, or stepping stone. That
is the organisation itself. Unless we have what I have called
an 'intraprise' to accommodate the full intrapreneurial variety,
we shall have no hope of realising our goals. So let me
in the next chapter, sketch out the kind of business organisation that managers need to develop.

12 How to develop an 'intraprise'

If the intrapreneur is to flourish, in all his guises, then there needs to be a form of organisation that will accommodate his varying attributes. Such an organisation I call the 'intraprise'. For, as with the 'intrapreneur', I am as much concerned with the organisation's inner form ('intra') as with its outer thrust ('prise').

In the view of business I have adopted here the corporation, or intraprise, exists to receive the intrapreneur. It is a receptacle, which incorporates, or accommodates imagination, intuition, organisation, assertiveness, flexibility, enthusiasm and activity. In that capacity, its shape or form is very different from that of the conventional family tree. It is multi-shaped, and three dimensional in form.

The holographic intraprise

I call the intraprise 'holographic' for two reasons. Firstly, it does have a much richer form than its skeletal predecessor, and is therefore much better appreciated in three dimensions than two. Secondly, to adapt William Blake's immortal words, its world can be seen through intrapreneurial grains of sand. In other words, as illustrated in Figure 12.1 there is:

- A NUCLEUS which has the originating power of the creative imagination.
- An EVOLVING ORGANISM that is an extension of the 'new designer's' unfolding and intuitive awareness.

- A formal STRUCTURE that accommodates and channels the ordered approach of the manager or leader.
- Autonomous PROFIT CENTRES through which entrepreneurs can assert themselves.
- An interactive NERVE CENTRE, enabling change agents to communicate, to learn, to change, and to adapt.
- A binding corporate CULTURE that contains the myths and the rituals, the social activities and the ceremonies, that animateurs nourish.
- The ENERGY sources, including power lines, transportation facilities, plant and equipment, recreation and sports facilities, that enable adventurers to channel their energies.

Figure 12.1 The Holographic Intraprise

The intrapreneur, therefore, whether he is thinking in terms of a small department or of a whole corporation, must ask himself the following range of questions:

- What is the nucleus of our business?
- How is our organism evolving?
- What formal structures do we require?
- Where are our profit centres?
- How do we foster experimentation and change?
- How is our cultural tapestry woven?
- Where does the physical energy lie?

Let me now elaborate.

The nucleus is the originating idea

How do you discover the nucleus of your business, function or department? The answer is not an easy one. For the nucleus should contain that originator's vision which so often gets lost in the cobwebs of history or in the entanglements of bureaucracy. The nucleus is composed of concentrated energy, the white heat of inspiration, the crucible of imagination.

Within Habitat–Mothercare's nucleus, for example, lies an image of a 'nation of shopkeepers', a vision of 'self-sufficiency' and a tradition of 'classical, functional design'. These have been powerfully, and imaginatively combined together. The resulting products, and corporate image, form the outcome. Conran's originating idea was and is Habitat–Mothercare's life source. To the extent that his vision is fully shared the company's products will be 'psychologically owned' by one and all. However, if the innovative nucleus is to be extended, as opposed to being merely shared by each activity, then something further is required. For example, Conran's design philosophy would need to infiltrate organisation development, if it was to become all pervading.

The sorts of questions managers need to ask themselves, with a view to imbibing or developing an innovative nucleus within their organisation are:

- What are our historic *origins* and *destiny?*
- What *image* are we projecting to the world?
- What fundamental *values* are we imparting?
- What is our underlying *product?*
- How will we *transform* our environment?
- What basis do we have for continued *innovation?*

In all cases, the questions may apply to a big company, a small department, or both, in turn.

The harmonic function stimulates development

The originating vision evolves, is developed and connected with emerging technological, market and human potential by the enabling, catalytic, harmonic function. Forming a part of product, market and organisation development, this function is a linking one. It links past with future, actual with potential, and one function or activity with another. It can be associated with the work of a research scientist, industrial designer, or organisation developer, each of who links actual with potential, in person or thing, product or market. The activity is represented better by dissolving and merging bubbles, or by interlocking hexagons, than by boxes and flow charts. It is manifested, in Mary Quant's organisation, where an intricate pattern of licensing arrangements links suppliers and distributors with Mary Quant designs. The designs themselves, of course, link Mary's own patterns of thought and imagination with market trends and consumer tastes. The harmonic function is reflected in joint ventures rather than acquisitions, in development rather than management, and in lateral rather than vertical connections. The questions managers need to ask themelves, therefore, include:

- Where are we in our organisational *evolution?*
- With what and whom are we *connected?*
- Where does our product, market and human *potential* lie?
- How can we *link* one form of *potential* with another?
- Where can we exercise and secure *mutual benefit?*
- Where is there scope for *joint ventures?*

- How can we *orchestrate* product, profit and risk sharing?
- How should we *develop* our 'intraprise'?

Structure grounds the organisation

For many people, both inside the organisation and out, the originating idea and harmonising function remain largely invisible. Often, we lack the vision and the sensitivity to imagine the former and to apprehend the latter. So it is the formal structure of the organisation and its tangible activities which strike us first. They ground the organisation making it appear, literally, down to earth.

The familiar organisation chart, the layers of authority, the specialised business functions, the delegated tasks and jobs, all help to concretise and to stabilise activity. In fact, the formal structure is to the business what the skeleton is to the body. It provides stability and firmness. Without our skeletal framework we would all collapse in a heap, no matter how active our minds or hearts.

Any large organisation, like ICI, needs such a structure, in order to maintain itself. But the ever present danger is that the structure, or bureaucracy, becomes overbearing, and pulls the organisation down. The questions that arise, in relation to structure, are familiar ones to most of us:

- What are our formalised *policies and procedures?*
- What explicit *plans and strategies* have been formulated for our business?
- What is our *formal structure,* including our lines of authority and responsibility?
- What *specialised* business *divisions,* functions or departments have we set up, including the component part of each?
- What formal *controls* have we established to ensure we conform to plan?
- What *lines of communication* have we established to co-ordinate activities effectively?
- What *responsibilities* to our stakeholders, within the company and without, have we delineated?

Enterprise turns product into profit

By virtue of organisation, the intraprise keeps itself in production. By virtue of enterprise, and through the acquisition of customers and resources, the business turns productivity into profitability. The innovative nucleus without entrepreneurial cells is like a new product without a champion. The harmonic function, divorced from the spirit of enterprise, is like an idea with potential, but without any prospects.

Entrepreneurial cells lie close to the customer and are powered by an acquisitive, achieving individual. They are fed by transactions, deals, ventures, and acquisitions that satisfy the individual's competitive and territorial instincts. Enterprise is dynamic, disruptive, acquisitive, expansive. While powered by individual will and emotion, it is channelled through lines of contact and influence. As in the case of Jack Dangoor, and his 'Advance Technology', enterprise is fleet footed, quick witted, well connected and individual centred.

Entrepreneurial cells lie at the cutting edge of the intraprise. They have sharp edges and will run smoothly if told how much of a market to slice off, when, but not how or where. More specifically, the questions to be asked of enterprise, are:

- How can we popularise the inventions of others, and when, so that we make a good *profit?*
- How do we get in the *best people?*
- How can we put the best *deal* together, involving what combination of people, or companies, and resources?
- How, and from whom, do we acquire the quantity of *finance* required?
- How much *risk* are we willing to take?
- How can we acquire, defend and expand our *power* base?
- What financial *incentive* can we provide our people with to ensure 100 per cent effort?
- How do we get in the *customers,* a lot of them, and fast?

Learning must be greater than the rate of change

Entrepreneurial cut and thrust, fuelled by strong emotional drive, must be accompanied by intelligent communications, if the business is to adapt, continually, to change. In fact, if learning is not greater than the rate of change, the intraprise will become extinct. So while the nucleus of the business innovates, and the harmonic function interrelates, management sets standards, enterprise yields profitable results, and the organisational nerve centre contains systems for adapting to change.

Adaptation is called for when novelty is in the air, and the key to such learning is information. The fluid organisation needs information, from within and without, to keep it in touch. The more variety and individuality there is in the environment the more information is required for us to keep tabs on things. Experimental units and project teams are required to adapt to changes.

This is exactly what has kept F International successfully going as a bespoke software house. The questions that Steve Shirley and we managers have to ask ourselves, therefore, are:

- Have we set up long-term plans, and also the systems for monitoring and *adapting* them?
- Have we developed loose organisational units that enable us to *learn* in unpredictable ways?
- Have we installed intelligent machines to *process information* and to structure adaptive responses?
- Have we recruited a variety of knowledge workers to provide *flexible* information and expertise?
- What systems and procedures have we established to attract freelancers, sub-contractors and *networkers?*
- What *task forces,* ad hoc groups, and project teams have we established, that can be quickly disbanded, as and when required?
- How do we encourage *experimentation* in individuals and in organisational units, as well as in research and development?

A binding culture compensates for non-stop change

Individual freedom and constant change have their limitations. Shared values, as well as ceremonies and rituals are also needed to bind people together. In their absence, the intraprise may fall apart. No formal systems will be able to establish the kind of esprit de corps that shared activities and popularly acclaimed stories create. Parties, badges, dramas and rituals can all play their part in creating a corporate culture that sucks people in. Nelli Eichner's Interlingua is full of such animated activities and events, many of them associated with the mainstream of her business.

Within a vibrant culture, like Interlingua's, it will not be difficult to identify such roles as hero (achievement through adversity), priest (the guardian of values) and storyteller. The culture will be a veritable tapestry of myth, ritual and anecdote, for all to share. For the animateur, there is no happiness like shared happiness. To the extent that management wants to establish a supportive culture, it will need to ask:

- How can we provide *social contact* between people, as employees, freelancers, customers or suppliers?
- How do we weave a rich *tapestry of myth,* anecdote, business dramas and fairy tales?
- How do we sustain a *climate* of romance and friendship, as well as scandal and feud?
- How do we establish supportive rites and rituals, and create *heroes* and binding values?
- How do we identify and publicise meaningful allegories, *stories* and precedents and encourage the people who pervade them?
- How do we provide access to a wide range of *group activity* at work and at leisure, among the members of our intraprise?
- How do we establish a *family* atmosphere within and alongside the company?

Ultimately there is physical activity

At the end of the day, however cohesive the culture, however quickly people learn, however enterprising the product champions, however well designed the organisation structure, however alert the new designers are to potential, however innovative the core idea, the business will produce nothing at all if there is no physical activity. Ultimately, it all starts and ends with energy.

Some of this energy, an increasing amount in modern times, is being supplied mechanically. But there will always need to be other energy that is supplied by people. Anita Roddick can take jet planes and fast cars to get her to places all over the globe, but without having a lot of stamina of her own, she would find it very difficult to keep going. We can be jet setting executives travelling the globe, but the ever more popular phenomenon of 'management by walkabout' demands personal and physical activity.

So, no matter how many company planes there are; no matter how good the surrounding transportation system, the following questions need to be asked:

- What facilities do we have to help members of the organisation keep themselves in good *physical shape?*
- Do we provide our people with the opportunity to eat *healthy food,* as well as take regular exercise?
- What facilities exist whereby people can *relax* in a quiet space, and to what extent are timetables flexible enough to allow this?
- Does the work involve a fair *balance* of mental and physical activity?

Conclusion

MATCHING INTRAPRENEUR AND INTRAPRISE
We have now covered the full spectrum of 'intrapreneuring' and 'intraprising' endeavour. The holographic organisation is the one that creates a match between individual

- imagination
- intuition
- organisation
- assertiveness

- flexibility
- animation
- activity;

intrapreneurial

- innovation
- design
- management
- entrepreneurship
- change-agency
- animateurship
- adventure;

intraprise

- nucleus
- organism
- structure
- cells
- nerve centre
- culture
- energy.

For all of us, time and space are vital dimensions for our development. In fact, the manager or consultant confined to a particular specialism or division, for an extended period of time, is severely handicapped. Similarly, the individual confined to a particular attribute of his personality, will remain similarly inhibited. Ironically, although there are seven paths of intrapreneurial development, each one is enriched by the other. To make things happen you require not only the physical energy to move people and things, but also other qualities to move them somehow, somewhere. In fact, there is nothing more magnificent than a rainbow arched across the sky, with its spectrum of colours fully visible.

In the final part of the book, I want to explore with you in detail how you develop, as an individual, in business.

Part IV

13 Developing in phases

In the course of becoming an intrapreneur, of one kind or another, you will develop in phases. John Harvey Jones did not become a leader overnight. He started his career as a trainee officer in the Navy. Steve Shirley did not become a manager of change all of a sudden. She started out, in her youth, as a programmer and troubleshooter before moving on to bigger and better things.

Bernard Lievegoed,[1] the Dutch organisational psychologist, says that we pass through three major stages in our lives: a time to learn, up till the age of twenty; a time to expand, between twenty and forty; and a time to grow wise, from forty onwards. In this penultimate chapter on your business individuality I want to focus on such phases of intrapreneurial development.

As the American biologist George Land[2] has said, we grow, qualitatively speaking, or we die, psychologically speaking. So you only realise your full intrapreneurial potential, whether as an animateur or an innovator, as an entrepreneur or an adventurer, if you successfully undergo life's transitions.

Your development path

The person who has most comprehensively charted our adult development is in fact the American researcher, Daniel Levinson, who wrote the widely-read *The Seasons of Man's*

Life.[3] Although his particular focus was on men in the course of their adult development, most of his findings would seem to apply equally to women.

Your development path, over the course of a lifetime, includes four phases, interspersed with transitions. These phases and transitions together comprise what Levinson calls your 'life structure'. In this chapter I want, firstly, to uncover this developmental life structure for a business individual, and, secondly, to reveal the general preconditions for healthy development.

Your underlying life structure

Your life structure is not a random set of events, like pebbles washed up on the shore. Rather, like threads in a tapestry, the events are woven into an encompassing design. Recurring themes help to unify the overall pattern of the tapestry. However, your lives differ widely in the nature and patterning of their specific elements.

Your life structure, then, evolves through a relatively orderly sequence during your adult years. It consists of alternating stable, structure building and transitional structure changing periods.

To construct anything, something else must be destructured and restructured. In human reproduction, an ovum and a sperm are joined to create a new being; but many others are left to die. The balance of nature is a mixture of destruction and creation. Both are essential to the harmony and evolution of individuals, organisations and societies.

In fact, at each phase of your development, a new balance has to be created between the forces not only of creativity and destruction, but also of youth and age, of masculinity and femininity and of separation and attachment.

The primary task of every stable period, then, is to build a life structure that reconciles those four sets of opposing forces in a new and appropriate way. You must make certain key choices, form a structure around them, and pursue your values and goals within that structure. A transitional period terminates the existing life structure and creates the possibility for a new one.

Your decision to 'stay put' within a stable period is not always based on commitment. It may stem from resignation, inertia, passive acceptance or controlled despair – a self restriction in the context of severe external constraints. This kind of surface stability marks the beginning of long term decline unless new factors intervene (perhaps in the next transitional period) and enable you to form a more satisfactory life structure.

The primary tasks of every transitional period are to question and to reappraise the existing structure, to explore various possibilities for change in yourself and in your world, and to move towards commitment to the crucial choices that form the basis for your new life structure in the ensuing stable period.

Your task in a developmental transition, therefore, is to terminate a time in your life; to accept the losses that termination entails; to review and evaluate the past; to decide which aspects of the past to keep and which to reject; and to consider your wishes and possibilities for the future. You are suspended between past and future, struggling to overcome the gap that separates them. Much from the past must be given up, separated from, cut out of your life; and there is much that can be used as a basis for the future.

In every transitional period, throughout the cycle of your life, the internal figures of Young and Old are modified and placed in a new balance. The end of the preceding period stimulates Old thoughts and feelings about being in a rut, rotting, coming to the brink of death. The start of a new period stimulates New thoughts and feelings about being reborn, making a fresh start, discovering fresh possibilities in oneself and new vistas in one's world.

The task in every transition is to create a new Young/Old integration appropriate to that time of life. With the change of eras there is normally an increase in the Old qualities of maturity, judgement, self awareness, magnanimity, integrated structure, breadth of perspective. But these qualities are of value only if they continue to be vitalised by the Young's energy, imagination, capacity for foolishness and fancy.

In summary, the most fundamental tasks of a stable period are to make firm choices, rebuild one's life structure and enhance one's life within it. Those of a transitional period are to question and reappraise the existing period, to search for new possibilities in oneself and in the world, and to modify the present structure enough for a new one to be formed.

Thus, for example, in young adulthood (thirties and forties), Terence Conran built up his Habitat chain. In midlife (forties and fifties) he began to reappraise his strategy, which resulted in a broadening out of his activity to encompass Mothercare, Richard Shops, and subsequently BHS. Thereafter, in this next phase of development, a new corporate structure – Storehouse – was created.

So much for your life structure. What about your life's phases?

The phases and transitions you need to undergo

Levinson divides the course of your life into four transitional periods, and four stable life structures, as can be seen in Table 13.1.

Table 13.1
Life phases

Age	Transitional period	Stable structure
17–22	Early adult transition	
22–28		Novice phase
28–33	Age thirty transition	
33–40		Settling down phase
40–45	Midlife transition	
45–52		Phase of renewal
52–57	Age fifty transition	
58–		The legacy phase

EARLY ADULT TRANSITION (17–22)

The first task, in your early adult transition, is to terminate your adolescent life structure, thereby leaving the pre-adult world behind you. This involves modifying existing relationships with important persons and institutions, as well as the self you formed in adolescence. Separations from family and schoolfriends are required as well as the loss of a certain degree of dependence.

The second task is to take a preliminary step into the adult world: to explore its possibilities, to imagine oneself as a participant in it, to make and test some tentative choices, before entering it.

The first task involves a process of termination, the second a process of initiation. Jack Dangoor, you may recall, mastered each one of them. Both are essential in a transitional period. Out of this opening transition emerges the young adult life structure, that is 'the novice phase'.

THE NOVICE PHASE (22–28)

Three major tasks, in your twenties, are crucial to your vocational and management development. These comprise the formation of your 'dream', of a suitable mentor relationship, and of an appropriate occupation. I shall start with the most important of these tasks, the uncovering of 'the dream'.

*forming a dream and giving it a place in the life structure

Your 'dream', like Conran's dream of self sufficiency and Mary Quant's dream of the black and white dancer, lend prolonged excitement and vitality to the novice's life. It is associated with the 'I am' feeling.

Your 'dream' may be modest like Nelli Eichner's ('There is no happiness like shared happiness') or heroic like Steve Shirley's ('I'm going to change the world'). It is usually vaguely defined, at first, and only very occasionally crystal clear; it may be a burning passion or a quiet guiding force, a source of inspiration or of gentle comfort. In dramatic terms, your 'dream' is your personal myth, an imagined drama in which you are the central character, a would-be hero or heroine engaged in a noble quest.

forming a dream

The vicissitudes and fate of the Dream have funda-mental qualities for adult development. In its primordial form, the Dream is a vague sense of self-in-adult-world. It has the quality of a vision, an imagined possibility that generates excitement and vitality.

At the start it is usually poorly articulated and only tenuously connected to reality, although it may contain concrete images such as winning the Nobel prize or making the national football team.

It may take dramatic form as in the myth of the hero: the great artist, business tycoon, athletic or intellectual superstar performing magnificent feats and receiving special honours. It may, alterna-tively, take the mundane forms that are not yet inspiring and sustaining: the excellent craftsman, the husband–father in a certain kind of family, the highly respected man of one's community.

Daniel Levinson, *The Seasons of Man's Life*[4]

Whatever its nature, as a young person you have the develop-mental task of giving the dream greater definition and finding ways of living it out. It makes a great difference in your growth whether your Novice phase is in tune with, and infused by, the 'dream', or opposed to it. If the 'dream' remains unconnected to your life it may simply die, and with it your sense of aliveness and purpose. For all our role models, from Conran to Roddick, their 'dreams' are indeed connected to their lives, and to their businesses.

Many of you, in fact, develop a conflict between your life direction expressing the 'dream' and another that is quite different. In your youth you may be pushed away from your 'dream' by your parents, by various external constraints, such as lack of money or opportunity, and by various aspects of your personality, such as guilt, passivity, competitiveness and special talents. You may thus succeed in an occupation that holds no interest for you.

Alternatively, if you do fulfil your 'dream' you will inevitably find, particularly as you approach midlife, that the hero of the 'dream' is only one of many figures in your life. To the extent that this figure plays predominant part in the evolution of the Novice phase, other parts of yourself tend to be neglected. For example, if you fulfil your 'dream' by becoming a millionaire you may neglect to develop the artistic side of your nature.

Inevitably, therefore, whether or not you work on and through your 'dream' in early adulthood, it will have to be reworked in later life. Mentor relationships are likely to help in that process. In fact the second task of your Novice phase lies therein.

*forming mentor relationships

In your early twenties, in particular, you stand to gain from an 'apprenticeship' with an appropriately more advanced, expert and authoritative 'mentor'. As the relationship evolves, you gain a fuller sense of your own authority and of your capability for autonomous, responsible action.

More specifically the mentor involved may act, firstly, as a teacher, serving to enhance your skills and intellectual development. Secondly, he may serve as a sponsor, using his influence to facilitate your advancement. Thirdly, he may act as a host and guide, welcoming you into a new occupational role and social world, and acquainting you with its customs, values, resources and cast of characters. Fourthly, the mentor may serve as an exemplar that you can admire and seek to emuluate.

The mentor has a fifth and final function, and this is developmentally the most crucial one: to support and facilitate the realisation of your dream. He fosters your development by believing in you, sharing the youthful 'dream' and giving it his blessing, helping to define your newly discovered self in its freshly discovered world, and creating space in which you can work on a life structure that contains the 'dream'.

For Mary Quant, for example, Terence Conran (teacher and exemplar), Archie Macnair (sponsor), and Alexander (guide and facilitator), all played such mentor roles.

*forming an occupation

In every period of your life, though, the developmental tasks are contrasting, even antithetical. Just as the 'Early adult transition' requires you both to terminate one era and to initiate the next, 'Entering the adult world' requires you both to explore freely and to make firm choices. This was very apparent for Jack Dangoor, as he simultaneously researched the watch market and set up his import–export business.

The exploratory stage requires you to 'hang loose', keeping your options open and avoiding strong commitments. To varying degrees, the outside world provides multiple possibilities. Also your own youthful vitality generates a sense of adventure and wonder, a wish to seek out all the treasurers of the new world you are entering.

At the same time, in your early to mid twenties, you must take on adult responsibilities and begin to make something of your life. Externally there are pressures to 'grow up', get married, enter an occupation, and lead a more organised life. Internally there are desires for stability and order, for roots, lasting ties, and for the fulfilment of core values.

Certain circumstances are more conducive to what Levinson terms 'forming' an occupation (as opposed to choosing one once and for all) over the course of the novice phase, than others. Supportive conditions, on the one hand, involve the granting of room to manoeuvre, and the freedom to make mistakes, together with the setting of clear limits and expectations. Challenging conditions, on the other hand, involve the setting of appropriate problem and opportunities for the individual to resolve. Jack Dangoor, through his family and himself, certainly had both.

No particular set of circumstances, though, is ideal. Forming an occupation, as has been indicated, is inherently paradoxical. If you make a strong occupational commitment in your early twenties, without sufficient exploration of external options and inner preferences, you often come to regret it later. On the other hand, if you don't make a commitment until your thirties, or never make one, you are deprived of the satisfaction of engaging in enduring work that is suitable for yourself and for society. So there is always a need to redress an occupational imbalance in later life.

At about 28, Levinson maintains the provisional qualities of the twenties begins to end and life becomes more serious, more for real. A voice within you says: 'If I am to change my life — if there are things in it I want to modify or exclude, or things missing I want to add — I must now make a start, for soon it will be too late.' John Harvey Jones made such a drastic choice a little earlier, when he left the Navy for ICI, at the age of 26.

The 'Age 30 transition', in fact, provides an opportunity to work on the flaws in your life structure formed during the previous period, and to create the basis for a more enduring future. For some people, according to Levinson, the transition proceeds smoothly. A person's life and work become modified and enriched.

However, for most, the transition takes on a more stressful form, just like the fraught transition from a 'Pioneering' to a 'Managed' organisation. You often fear that you can move neither forward or back. The integrity of your 'enterprise' is in serious doubt. Steve Shirley must have had such doubts in her stressful early years.

As this Age 30 transition extends itself, you move towards new choices or recommit yourself to existing ones. A great deal hinges on these choices. If they are well made — from the point of view of your 'dream', values, talents, possibilities — they provide the basis for a relatively satisfactory second, adult life structure. This was the case, for example, for Anita Roddick. If the preparatory work has been poorly done and the new structure is flawed, life in 'Settling down' will become increasingly painful.

THE SETTLING DOWN PHASE (32–40)

In the 'Settling down' phase you have two important tasks. Firstly, you must try to establish a niche in society, to anchor your life and work more firmly, to develop competence in a chosen field, and to become a valued member of a world you in turn value. Secondly, you have the task of striving to 'make it', to advance, to progress according to some inner or outward looking timetable. Harvey Jones consolidated his position in manufacturing industry and Anita Roddick in naturally based cosmetics.

Establishing a niche involves digging in, forming an occupation and pursuing your interests within a prescribed pattern. This is the initial step in 'Settling down'. You need a relatively ordered, stable life, in order to become established in your life and work.

Working at advancement involves striving to succeed, moving onward and upward, progressing according to a pre-ordained schedule. Whereas the first task – establishing a niche – contributes to the stability and order of a defined structure, the second – 'making it' – involves a progression within the structure.

The 'Settling down' life structure, then, gives certain of your aspirations and relationships a prominent place, while requiring that others be made secondary or put aside altogether. It may, depending on the case in point, permit expression of many or few aspects of yourself.

A relatively integrated structure has a few central elements which serve as focal points for the structure as a whole, while other peripheral elements enrich and expand the structure. For example, Steve Shirley created a structure for flexibility and freedom (focal points) and had professional competence and some acquired business acumen (peripheral elements) to go with it.

---

second life structure

The underlying task is to 'settle for' a few key choices, to create a broader structure around them, to invest oneself fully in the various components of the structure – such as work, family, community – and to pursue long range goals and plans within it. An individual has a stronger sense of urgency to 'get serious', to be responsible, to decide what is truly important and to shape his life accordingly.

Daniel Levinson, *The Seasons of Man's Life*[5]

To the extent, however, that you want order and stability you must be ready to moderate your upward striving which may rock your personal and familial boat. Nelli Eichner was a good case in point. Conversely, an individual who wants desperately to make a mark, to attain great heights of power, virtue or achievement, cannot afford to place great value on stability. That applies, for example, to Dangoor and Conran.

The imagery of the ladder, finally, is central to the settling down phase. It reflects the interest in advancement and affirmation so central to this period. By 'ladder', Levinson refers to all dimensions of advancement – increases in social rank, income, power, fame. The ladder has both objective and subjective aspects. It reflects the realities of the external world, but it is also defined by you in terms of your own meanings and strivings – be they physically, socially, technologically, economically, aesthetically, or culturally circumscribed.

THE MIDLIFE TRANSITION (40–45)

At around 40, when you reach the top rung of your early adult ladder, you have to reappraise the ladder itself. It is not just a matter of evaluating how well you have done within the current definitions of success and failure. You have to question the basic meanings of success and failure, including the value of the ladder.

In reworking your 'dream', then, you need to modify the meaning of the ladder, to evaluate your success or failure in more complex terms, and to give more emphasis to the quality of experience, to the intrinsic value of this work and productivity, and their meaning to yourself and to others. Thus, for Nelli Eichner, shared happiness took precedence over business success.

For the great majority, according to Levinson's research into people from all walks of life, mid-life transition spans a period of struggle. The individuals he investigated began to question nearly every aspect of their lives, feeling they could not continue as before. Past and future coexist in the present, but the individual suffers from corrosive doubt as to whether they can be joined.

During the period from 40 to 45, then, you need to reduce your heavy investment in the external world. To do the work of reappraisal you must turn inward. You have to discover what your turmoil is about, and where it hurts. Having been overly engaged with worldly struggles, you need to be more engaged with yourself. Hence the recent wave of interest, generally amongst the maturer business enterprises, and specifically with Harvey Jones, in 'corporate culture', that inner manifestation of a corporation's other being.

---

inner mapping

The 'geographical study' is a mapping expedition in a territory often experienced as a desert, with long stretches of sand enlivened by occasional oases. The traveller discovers that some of the perceived water holes are mirages, others real, and that the territory contains far more resources than he has been able to see. Slowly he learns how to look below the surface and to make use of the treasures he finds there . . .

Daniel Levinson *The Seasons of Man's Life*[6]

THE MIDLIFE PHASE OF RENEWAL (45–52)

Every transition presents you with the opportunity of moving towards an integration of each of the four sets of polarities – young/old; destruction/creation; masculine/feminine; attachment/separateness – that I have already identified.

At midlife, however, the demand for integration is particularly strong. The energy and vigour of youthful aspiration needs to be tempered by the durability and perspective of seasoned wisdom. The 'destructive' features of cut and thrust need to be counterbalanced by the 'creative' features of development and renewal.

The power of 'masculine' analysis and competitiveness needs to be tempered by 'feminine' intuition and co-operation. Attachment to self centred, material goals needs to be re-balanced, through a growing separation from tangible aspirations, towards a more spiritually oriented search for self actualisation.

Every life structure, Levinson maintains, gives high priority to certain aspects of yourself and neglects others. In midlife these neglected aspects seek particularly urgent expression. Internal voices that have been silent for years now clamour to be heard. You hear the voice of an identity prematurely rejected, of a goal lost sight of or not pursued, of a valued connection given up in acquiescence to authority, of an internal figure who wants to be an academic or an entrepreneur. You must learn to listen to these voices and decide consciously what part you will give them in your life.

In fact, the great developmental task of this era – for an organisation, perhaps, as well as for an individual – is not to retire early from worldly responsibilities but to seek a new balance between power and love. It is critically important, both to society and to yourself in middle adulthood, that you accept the burdens and the pleasure of responsibility, that you learn to exercise authority with more wisdom and compassion, and that you tolerate the guilt and pain that are the price of the self conscious use of power. All this our intrapreneurs have come to terms with, especially Conran, Harvey Jones and Roddick.

In midlife, then, you should consciously set out to re-balance the needs of self and society. You can develop greater wisdom if you are less focused on the acquisition of specific skills, knowledge and rewards, and more focused on the intrinsic pleasure of work and of having more individualised, loving relationships. While you might still enjoy the tangible rewards of power and influence, in some shape or form, you gain even greater satisfaction from empowering others.

AGE 50 TRANSITION INTO MATURITY, AND THE LEGACY PHASE (52–)
The imagery of the 'Legacy' begins to emerge in your midlife transition. Your legacy, according to Levinson, is what you pass on to future generations. It includes material possessions, creative products, business enterprises, influences on others. People, he says, differ enormously in their views about what constitutes a legacy. Although the real value of any such legacy is impossible to measure, in his mind it defines, to a large degree, the ultimate value of your life.

In every era, in fact, you have the need and the capability to generate a legacy. But it is in the final phase of life that the task of building one acquires its greatest developmental significance. It can also become your ultimate vision, or source of profound creativity.

The creative impulse is not merely to make something. It is to bring something into being, to give birth, to generate life. In that sense, as they enter their fifties and sixties, Conran's desire to infuse retailing with good design, and Harvey Jones' desire to transform Britain's industrial base, both intensify.

Negotiating your life's course

There is no guarantee that you will successfully negotiate your life's course, thereby developing as an individual, and as an intrapreneur. For whatever intrapreneurial path you are following or forging – be it a path of adventure, happiness, change, enterprise, leadership, development or creativity – you will need certain attributes.

YOUR PATHFINDING ATTRIBUTES
There are five particular attributes that you need to possess. Without them you will fail to negotiate life's transitions. In

other words you will remain stuck in a particular phase, and fail to develop your full intrapreneurial potential. These specific attributes are:

- Capacity for insight
- Possession of foresight
- Tolerance of uncertainty
- Willingness of risk
- Courage to change

As a developing intrapreneur, firstly, you need sufficient insight into yourself, at a particular stage of your life, to realise that you are undergoing a phase of development. This kind of insight requires a certain sensitivity to needs emerging from within. It also often means discarding roles and behaviours expected from without. Thus Conran turned from a designer into a more wide-ranging 'corporate architect'.

Secondly, as an intrapreneur successfully engaged in your own self development, you need sufficient foresight to avoid going down blind alleys. You can somehow tell which path of development offers the greatest potential for personal and business growth, as was the case for Jack Dangoor when he teamed up with Ferranti.

Thirdly, you are able to tolerate uncertainty in that you allow your life to move in fits and starts. Development, as we have already seen, is not a smooth and continuous process. Thrusts of energy are often followed by periods of uncertainty and retrenchment. Progress is usually slow, and seldom steady. Pathfinders, like Steve Shirley, know and can accept this, even though it makes their lives uncomfortable.

You, are prepared fourthly, to take 'psychological' risks whereby you are willing to give up personally restrictive practices. In other words, for example, Steve Shirley was willing to give up her job – temporarily entering a vocational backwater – because of the developmental prospects that arose. A secondment to a new venture, or to a community project, is a typical case in point.

Fifthly, if you are engaged in intrapreneurial self development, you have the courage to change your closely held beliefs, in the light of new information and experience, and also dare to include others in your pathfinding, whose values are fundamentally different from their own. Finally, you have the inclination to set out on your own, despite personal or family misgivings, in order to pursue your 'Dream'.

CREATING YOUR OWN LIFE

If these are the general attributes of successful intrapreneurs, what are the particular, and creative, steps that you have to take in negotiating a life transition? In other words, what is the creative process in which successfully developing business individuals engage? What emerges from your capacity for insight, and foresight, from your tolerance of uncertainty, willingness to take personal risks, and from your courageous accommodation of change?

How do you manage the personal transition from an immature intrapreneurial state, like that of a trainee manager or salesman, to that of a business executive or entrepreneur? The general rules for each and every developmental point are set out in Table 13.2.

Table 13.2
Managing personal transition

The creative process	The process of transition
PREPARATION Gathering impressions and images	ANTICIPATION Imagining oneself into the next phase of life and work
INCUBATION Letting go of certainties	INCUBATION/SEPARATION Lettings go of an outlived identity
ILLUMINATION Leaping into the unknown	EXPANSION Being swept along in a fast current
REVISION Conscious restructuring, and editing of creative material	INCORPORATION Reflection on, and integration of new aspects of one's life and work

Whether you are negotiating the 'early adult', 'age thirty', 'midlife', or 'age fifty' transition, the following common and creative process applies:

ANTICIPATION, firstly, like the gathering of impressions and images, involves preparing to meet a prospective transition rather than becoming lost in everyday detail, or in vague procrastination. Intrapreneurs who are particularly well prepared have:

- collected the skills they are likely to require (e.g. Dangoor's technical and commercial skills)
- developed a picture, an image of how things will be (e.g. Conran's image of self sufficiency)
- couched such a picture in positive terms, and enthusiastically pursued it (e.g. Eichner's 'shared happiness')

Secondly, SEPARATION AND INCUBATION: as you painfully let go of old certainties, you give up increasingly destructive aspects of your old self to form space for newly creative aspects. So an expanded identity replaces the previous and restricted one. Outgrown social roles and 'shoulds', along with old fears and handicapping defences, are re-examined in the light of new possibilities for integrating your personality in the stage to come. Thus Steve Shirley outgrew her reaction against 'bureaucracy', to further her dream.

Thirdly, as you leap into the physical, economic or psychological unknown, you plunge into new territory of one kind or another, often experiencing heightened sensations through this process of EXPANSION. Your senses are thereby enlivened, your insights quicken, and their focus often becomes selective. However, having dared to get your feet wet in a new stream, you may well be swept along in such a fast current of events that they become temporarily out of control. Conran is a good case in point, with his successive and opportunistic mergers.

Finally, after the hurly burly of expansion, there is a dormant period in which you are able consciously to restructure yourself and your world. Through this process of incorporation, you reflect on what has changed, and integrate the meaning of these changes into your philosophy of life and work. It is important to allow time for the whole of yourself to absorb and clear, and to allow for your batteries to be recharged.

Summary

There is a series of four life phases – structure forming – and four life transitions – structure changing – that underpin your intrapreneurial development. In each of these phases, duly interspersed with transitions, the polarities of creation and destruction, youth and age, masculinity and femininity, separation and attachment, need to be newly and appropriately balanced.

If you are to develop intrapreneurially you will pass through four stages (combinations of phases and transitions): exploration, consolidation, renewal, and individuation. Each of them needs to contain different resolutions of the above mentioned polarities.

In order to negotiate these stages successfully you need to anticipate the future, separate from the past, expand outwards without overdue self control, and incorporate yourself into the evolving situation.

In my final chapter I want to weave the developmental strands into the seven intrapreneurial characters, and review the practical implications for your life and work.

References

1 Lievegoed, B., *Phases*, Rudolf Steiner Press, 1979,
2 Land, G., *To Grow or to Die*, Wiley, 1986
3 Levinson, D., *The Seasons of Man's Life*, Knopf, 1978
4 Levinson, D., op.cit.
5 Levinson, D., op.cit.
6 Levinson, D., op.cit.

14 Becoming an intrapreneur

In the last chapter we uncovered the main phases of adult development, together with the intervening transitions. We discovered, as a result, four developmental stages of exploration, consolidation, renewal and individuation.

In other words, although you each have a different intrapreneurial path to forge, or to follow, each one of your paths will be crossed by somewhat predictable demands at particular stages of your life. If you successfully negotiate your life's transitions, responding positively to such demands, you will progressively round out your intrapreneurial personality, but still operate from a unique individual base.

The outcome of such cumulative and individual development will now be described. In each case an immature intrapreneurial form, one that is narrow and shallow, grows into a mature individual, whose intrapreneurial form is now broad and deep. In the process a simple one-dimensional business individuality grows into a more complex, multidimensional variety, whereby, for example, a specialist manager becomes a versatile business leader.

The intrapreneurial life cycle

There is a natural cycle of development, then, that applies to all intrapreneurs, at least in an approximate way. In fact, if you are to 'mature' as an adult, in the best sense of the word, you need to develop through four stages, incorporating both developmental phases and transitions.

EXPLORATION

In your youth, from your late teens to late twenties, you need to explore, to experiment and to take risks – just like the pioneering enterprise.

CONSOLIDATION

In your early adulthood you need to settle down into more of a routine, to establish yourself and to specailise. Thus in the period between your late twenties and thirties you can model yourself on the conventionally managed organisation.

RENEWAL

Then as you enter midlife, in your forties, you have to change direction – that is to broaden your horizons. More often than not you need to help yourself by helping others in one capacity or another. You become involved in the conscious development of yourself, of other people, or of products or markets in the broadest sense.

INDIVIDUATION

Finally, as you mature, you tap the true centre of your being and become, for the first time, your true self. In the process you realise your youthful dream.

The developing intrapreneur

We shall now chart your intrapreneurial path – that is one of the seven varieties – through an actual or prospective organisation. To enable you to do this I shall be drawing on the examples of seven organisationally based intrapreneurs. You will be able to compare and contrast these 'lesser mortals' with the 'greater' role models whom you have already come across.

The middle-sized engineering company from whom these seven individuals are drawn has set out to develop its intrapreneurial base in order to adapt to a rapidly changing market-place in the 1980s. Though the names and some places have been disguised, in the interests of confidentiality, I hope the reality will shine through. I have called the company Hydra and its key subsidiary Tapol Engineering.

Let me begin, then, with the corporate entrepreneur, and his counterpart, the animateur. In each case I shall review the kind of person you are, the intrapreneurial position you might occupy within an organisation, the rewards you may seek, and the way you are likely to develop.

****
Entrepreneur and Animateur
****

Enterprise is back in fashion. There has been a massive swing over the past five years from a bureaucratic, managerial approach to a dynamic, entrepreneurial one. Don Rowlands (see below) is such an ENTREPRENEUR within an existing organisation.

On the one hand Don represents a stepping back into the nostalgia of our imperial past. We yearn for the entrepreneurial spirit that carried forward the industrial revolution. On the other hand it represents a genuine attempt to rejuvenate moribund organisations and communities.

Accompanying the resurgence of entrepreneurship is the renewed concern for 'shared values'. Whereas the entrepreneur is rugged and thrusting, the so-called 'animateur' creates shared values by means of a developed 'corporate culture'. Ken Jones is an Australian version of such an 'ANIMATEUR' in Hydra.

For the youthful company, and for the corporation which is attempting to rejuvenate itself, aggressive entrepreneurship and communally shared values go hand in hand. The one divides and the other unites. Let me now elaborate on each.

Are you an ENTREPRENEUR?

The qualities of the entrepreneur are to a large extent instinctive and therefore difficult to cultivate. However, through appropriate challenges and support, mentorship and coaching, you can develop entrepreneurially, within an organisation, if you have the innate tendencies in the first place. Those of you who scored highly on category (e) in the spectral inventory are likely candidates. And you don't quite have to be a Jack Dangoor!

What qualities, then, does such an 'intrapreneur' have? To what extent do you have them yourself? How can you identify them in others? Let us investigate, through Don Rowlands.

DON ROWLAND   *ENTREPRENEUR*
BUSINESS DEVELOPMENT MANAGER

I was brought up by my grandparents. My mother died in childbirth. I went to a British boarding school at 10 and tried hard to make it have no effect on me. I strongly objected to all the razzmatazz – the pinstriped trousers and all that.

I left school at 19 and after loafing about for a year went on to university in Wales. I thoroughly enjoyed the university life and hated the chemical engineering I studied. When I was young I was interested in history, but I knew I couldn't make a living from it. I recognised, though, that chemical engineering was a useful tool. Having been sponsored at university by a large company, I expected to be sent to Singapore, or something like that. At 22 or 23 that is the sort of thing you were looking for. Instead I was sent to their research lab at Sunbury on Thames!

Young salesman

So, after a short stint with the large company I joined a much smaller one. They produced gas from oil. The day after I arrived people discovered gas in the North Sea. That was a good thing for me, because it induced great panic in the firm. That made life exciting. We rushed around trying out all sorts of new processes. I was involved on the development side. Twenty-two months worth of enthusiasm.

It was fun, but I wasn't getting enough exposure to clients. Also I wasn't involved with problems at source. I could ask what and how, but not why. So I accepted an offer to work for a large engineering company. I was 26 at the time. The job took me around the world, and gave me total freedom to work on my own. I got very involved in selling in the Far East, and, by the age of 29, applied for the job as sales manager for Africa. 'Stuff and nonsense', they told me. 'You're not old enough.' So I left.

It so happened that Cratex Technologies approached me in the late sixties. They were looking for a proposal engineer. I said I wanted to be a rep. They took me on and sent me to the West Country. I really enjoyed it. It set the old adrenalin flowing. I like the solitariness of the rep's life and the challenge of knocking on doors, selling plant to people who didn't know you. You'd see people, at 9.30 in the morning, who had just had a fight with their wife, and you had to bring them round. I could have been a rep all my life. It's the completeness of the role.

You're your own company. You have an organisation behind you that you cajole and batter. In fact the company, rather than the customer, is your biggest battle. But Cratex got taken over, two years after I joined, and I found the new regime much too stifling.

Becoming an entrepreneur

I was hired by the Tapol company to take on overseas sales. I was 34. I started looking into the Middle East. It was the place to be at the time. I travelled around Saudi, Iran, Libya, Egypt and the States. I was learning on the job how to handle international finance. It hadn't occurred to me before that it could present problems. I used to be out of the country 200 days a year. In 1976–1981 I did a lot of profitable work in the Middle East, before things began to turn sour. By 1982 the Arab world was running out of money. The British industrial market for contract work was also collapsing. I needed a change.

Business development

So I was given the job of setting up a technically oriented Development Group. I insisted on being able to pick my own people. I grabbed a sales manager and two engineers. One of the draughts-men was brilliant and confused. Something had to be done about him quick, or he'd leave.

I also insisted on a location remote from the centre. We needed to be set in a different world, worrying about tomorrow's problems. We needed the freedom, even to fail. People don't need manag-ing. You just have to set them a challenging task, with a time schedule and an incentive. I also wanted to get my people to relate to one another. The atmosphere had to be informal and the numbers small. Finally, I felt sure that what we did had to be market-led. Things went very well. We had 12 months of great enthusiasm and excitement. But after a year I became dispensable. I was brought in to Hydra's head office at the beginning of 1986, as overall Business Development Manager.

The spirit of enterprise

My new role is to infuse the company with a spirit of enterprise, and to turn that spirit into energy! That's a nice hunter role ... When I was leaping around in the Middle East, in my twenties and thirties, I was geared up for business. Success was an obsession. Leaping about all over the place I was turned on by immediate and profitable opportunities.

Now I'm 46. The late forties and fifties is about bringing on other people. Developing people, and businesses, is also about making connections. You recognise people have three strengths and then you look for a fourth that connects the other three. The person probably hasn't thought about it him-self.

Do companies RECRUIT you, as an entrepreneur?

Most people believe that no self-respecting entrepreneur will join a large organisation. That is only a half truth. After all, it may take a prospective entrepreneur like you, many years before you are ready to take the plunge. Moreover, there are many shades of entrepreneurship.

Some entrepreneurs may find the balance of risk and security offered by an autonomously structured corporation more acceptable than a business of their own. In a go-ahead company there will inevitably be a number of opportunities for entrepreneurs who can recognise a 'main chance' and also make and take one.

The areas in which entrepreneurship. is particularly encouraged are in merchandising, in sales, in new ventures, and in the general management of fast moving products and services.

How do you REWARD entrepreneurs?

Entrepreneurs are not motivated to climb up the corporate ladder in the conventional sort of way. In fact the entrepreneurial path is by nature circuitous rather than direct. As part of your wheeling and dealing, as an entrepreneur, you need to be able to step sideways, or move in a zigzag path, rather than stick to the straight and narrow.

An an entrepreneur, like Don Rowlands, you love to overcome obstacles and to take calculated and emotionally thrilling risks. Your life and workstyle are full of ups and downs, and of mistakes from which you are able to learn. Each new territory lost or (preferably) gained is a landmark or milestone in your dramatic journey.

As an entrepreneur you need to be given the rope either to hang yourself or to climb commercial mountains. You need capital both as a form of recognition and as a means to acquire personal freedom. You want to achieve the targets that you have set yourself and to be rewarded directly and financially for your accomplishments.

The entrepreneurial organisation you are looking for will not only offer you scope for financial gain, but will also encourage new ventures within which you can take an equity stake.

How do you DEVELOP as an entrepreneur?

As an entrepreneur, you do not develop by attending formal training courses. You need to be set, rather, appropriate personal and business challenges to which to respond. You also need to be provided with coaches and mentors who can not only live up to your entrepreneurial expectations, but also supersede them. Your 'dream' is to be rich and powerful!

In your youth you are likely to find the most opportunities in marketing, or else in championing a particular product or service in any one of the other functions. Travel to far-flung places and rewards directly related to your achievements are likely to enhance your performance, as an itinerant salesman or market trader.

In your thirties you should have the opportunity of managing a profit centre or semi-autonomous function in your own particular way. Challenge needs now to be accompanied, as it was for Don Rowlands, by growing territory and responsibility, as an entrepreneur.

In midlife entrepreneurs like some of you, and Don, should be broadening your terms of reference. Instead of being preoccupied only by money and markets you should also be widening your field of concern to encompass, to a much greater extent, the development of people and organisations.

This is a natural time for you to enter a development function, without losing your marketing or financial touch. Such a role would also serve to broaden the base of personnel or R&D department, with you as a business developer.

Finally, as you are fully mature, you might become involved in business renewal, through which the transformation of the comany, its product line, and its overall direction may be achieved. This is a role that Don Rowlands is now playing in Hydron, as he becomes his ultimate intrapreneurial self, embodying the spirit of enterprise.

What about, then, your 'other half', the animateur?

Are you an ANIMATEUR?

Because women have traditionally played a less influential

part than men in business life the entrepreneur has gained more credence than the animateur. In fact I had to borrow the word animateur from the French. You may be such an intrapreneur if you scored highly on category (g) in the spectral inventory.

As an animateur you are not a cartoonist, but, in the original context, a person who 'animates' individuals and groups within a particular locality. You accomplish this not only through your own charm and enthusiasm but also by drawing on your corporate and cultural heritage. Both Nelli Eichner (Czech by birth) at Interlingua and Ken Jones (an Australian) at Hydra have been good cases in point.

KEN JONES   *ANIMATEUR*
MANAGING DIRECTOR, HYDRA,
(AUSTRALIA)

I was born in Australia and grew up there. I was, and still am, a gregarious person. I love people.

Apprentice craftsman

I went to a technical high school, which was what one did in those days. I don't know why, but I was always keen on making things. My father was a banker, but my grandparents were in shipbuilding. I guess I had the sea in my blood. So I decided to take a cadetship at the naval dockyard in Sydney. A year before I finished my apprenticeship I applied for three jobs and got them all. I took the one at Topal because it was on my bus route. I've been there ever since.

I was heavily exposed to teams of construction engineers from some of the bigger companies. To watch those skilled operators put things together, and screw the locals for every cent in the process, was quite a learning, and nauseating, experience.

Skilled operator

At the time Australia was putting up a lot of power

stations. By 1967 I had become chief design engineer. About that time we got our first order for a condensate polishing plant. As I knew nothing about the technology I had to come over to the UK, the fount of all wisdom at the time. Afterwards I went back and engineered the plant.

Eventually our MD retired and Rob Hurst took over from him. He wanted to reorganise things in Asia, and he appointed my former boss as MD of the South East Asian operation. I then became contracts director, at the age of 37. It didn't really change much. I was still the technical chief. Rob kept a very firm hand on the costing. That was, and still is, his strong point. I still concentrated on the technical aspects, though I obviously acquired a reasonable knowledge of how to run a contracting outfit.

Becoming an animateur

Until two years ago I had a technical, management role. Suddenly I was stuck into managing and motivating people in a wide range of cultural settings. I was appointed MD. The only thing I've done of real significance is to restructure the Malaysian operation into a joint venture with a local partner. I get on with the locals. I trust them and they trust me. In my technical role I'd got to see a fair bit of Malaysia. I'd been out there a lot. Other people would make lightning visits and try to negotiate deals in British fashion, not taking local factors into account.

The thing about Malaysia is that it's not homogenous. The Malays make up the majority of the population and they're a relaxed people. The Chinese control commerce. The Indians are the traders. Although the country is generally a happy one, just below the surface there are conflicts. You have to take account of them. There are also all sorts of funny regulations you need to be aware of. We're coming in as a foreign company, which is 51 per cent Malay owned. Our Chairman is Chinese but our Malay Operations Director is also on the Board. You cannot do business the way you do it at home.

Indonesia, Thailand, Singapore, Hong Kong. Each is another story. If I've achieved anything it's getting a higher profile for Hydra in these countries, and I haven't made too many enemies. Whereas Rob's thing is finance mine is people and marketing.

Generating a community spirit

In time I can see myself generating a community spirit, within the company, that reaches beyond Australia into our operations in South East Asia. After all, Australia should be the gateway to the East.

When I was a child I was a sociable character, within my small group of friends. I can see how, over time, my social circle has become progressively larger, and larger. Within Hydra I feel we should be cultivating a worldwide community of interests.

Do organisations RECRUIT animateurs?

Animateurs are more likely to be found in America or in Italy than in the UK. In Britain, to the extent that they are about, they are more likely to be women than men, and more often – among the ranks of management – from Wales or Ireland than from Scotland or the southern part of England. However, there will be many exceptions to these rules, and you may well be one of them.

Animateurs are most likely to be found amongst the sales force, amongst the secretarial staff, or amidst those individuals in personnel or in operations who are seen to be natural and gregarious, 'people people'. In fact, in Britain at the present time, with the growing emphasis on 'customer care', animateurs are in ever-increasing demand. British Rail, British Airways and Barclays Bank are just three examples of companies which have rapidly developed their emphasis on service.

However, for any animateur – or entrepreneur for that matter – to be worth their salt, there has to be more to them than first meets the eye. For example the 'people person' must have that element of spunk and self-discipline that drives her purposefully on. That is what makes a Nelli Eichner stand out from the gregarious crowd.

How do you REWARD animateurs?

As an animateur you seek out a social circle to which to belong, whether or not it is entirely of your own making. The last thing you want is to be promoted into a position of isolation from your friends, colleagues and workmates, and from the product or service which matters to you. That is why Ken Jones had such mixed feelings about his first promotion.

However, if you are ambitious, you will want to broaden your circle of contacts progressively. This was clearly apparent for Nelli Eichner at Interlingua.

As an animateur you will be intent on bringing your practical and social skills to bear on situations, and you will be frustrated if prevented from doing so. You are rewarded not by individual recognition, but by recognition of the group in which you may have become a leading influence.

In fact, the reason that cooperative enterprises are more widespread in Italy or Spain than in Britain is because of the gregarious, Mediterranean influence. Cooperative achievement come naturally to the animateur. Although Nelli Eichner was undoubtedly the queen bee in her organisation she thrived on the shared accomplishments of her co-workers.

How do you DEVELOP as an animateur?

In your youth you will welcome the opportunity of meeting warmhearted people, and of working with people and things you really care about. Like Ken Jones or Nelli Eichner you are more of a craftsman than a technologist or professional. You learn best from people with whom you feel a natural rapport. Any training programme you go on has to be fun and friendly if it is to achieve the desired effect. Your 'dream' is to be happy.

As you enter young adulthood, in your thirties, you need to broaden the base of your activities and relationships, becoming a skilled operator in technical and social terms. The roles of a supportive coach, and an admired mentor, are particularly important for you at this stage.

In midlife you need to broaden out even further, beyond the relatively limited circle of the sales, production or personnel activity in which you might have been working. A natural development is from production or sales to divisional or company animateur, as has been the case for Ken Jones at Hydra. The corporate culture should both encourage you to broaden out and also provide you with the 'family' support you need in the course of making such a transition. Moreover, your enthusiasm and charm, rather than your dynamism or authority, will still remain to the fore.

Finally, as you approach maturity, you develop the potential to create a new and powerful culture in your organisation. That is what Nelli achieved and it is something to which Ken aspires. Such a corporate culture may be more in tune with the times than the one you inherited. You, in your turn, will come to be your ultimate self and embody the spirit of community.

So we can see the way in which, between the two of you as entrepreneur and animateur, you build up the base of your business. Enterprising cells and a cohesive culture are now in place. Autonomy and entrepreneurship, combined with shared values, are your joint creation. The net result is a profitable and growing business as well as contented customers and employees.

It is also apparent that, as you develop towards maturity, the scope, if not the essential nature of your individual role, changes. It becomes more broadly based and more deeply founded. In other words you absorb, if you open yourself to growth and development, some of the individual and intrapreneurial attributes that characterise others around you.

However, though Peters and Waterman may wish otherwise, a developing business needs more than its primal, instinctive duo. The bigger and more complex the business the greater the need for the leader and for the change agent, for the Harvey Joneses and for the Steve Shirleys of this world.

****

****
Business Leader and Change Agent
****

As a business evolves from a pioneering enterprise to a managed organisation so it requires additional heroes and heroines. No longer do entrepreneur and animateur dominate the show. The world has grown too complex for you two alone. Hence Western Germany and Japan supersede the United States, Australia or Hong Kong as models of industrial efficiency and effectiveness.

The era between the fifties and the eighties was dominated – in the industrialised nations at least – by the managed economy and by the managed organisation. The true hero of the managed organisation, that is the person with cut and thrust, is neither the manager nor the classical entrepreneur but a different 'intrapreneur', and that is the agent of change.

The business leader, believe it or not, is the 'heroine' of the managed organisation. His or her role is to provide coherence and integration, in the way that Harvey Jones has done and Bert Hammil is doing (see page 233 below).

The Japanese realise this all too well, seeing their managers as financial midwives, stewards of the company's resources, and agents of reconciliation, co-ordination and integration. Because we in the West have tended to get the managerial role wrong we have often ended up with 'paralysis by analysis'.

As we have seen, the entrepreneur and animateur have important parts to play in the managed organisation, but not the primary ones. They occupy the wings rather than the centre field, creating and nurturing new business ventures.

The main thrust is provided by agents of change who push out new products, and carve out new markets, by creating new systems and methods of organisation. Coherence and purpose are provided by the business leader, acting as the force of integration and co-ordination. He or she provides, or maintains, the underlying structure of the organisation. Let me now elaborate, beginning with the agent of change.

Are you a CHANGE AGENT?

The scope for the change agent is rapidly growing in today's managed organisations. In fact Harvey Jones at ICI called for such heroic individuals to take the company into the future. Typically they can be found in research, in computer programming and management services, in management training, in marketing, and amongst the more progressive functional managers. Steve Shirley and Tom Preen are both good cases. If, in the spectral inventory, you scored highest in category (f), you may well be one yourself.

TOM PREEN   *AGENT OF CHANGE*
MANAGER, TAPOL DEVELOPMENT

My father was a diplomat. I was born in Germany and we moved from place to place. I never stood still. You know, I believe that you should never be in a fixed position for too long. Every so often you need to change, for no particular reason, but just for change's sake. I was a child of the sixties. A flower child. I was into palmistry, graphology, and ley lines. All those fringe things. I've also always been interested in old churches. I'm a curious sort of person.

I used to get involved in endless discussions at College. I did pure chemistry and got interested in the inorganic part. The organic side of chemistry was a pain in the arse. It didn't suit my brain. It was too abstract. As soon as I was unable to imagine how something would react or respond I would feel anxious. The thing with inorganic chemistry is that you can predict reactions. Things fit together easily. I used to love fixing radios when they were built out of valves. When microchips took over they lost their appeal. I could no longer take them apart. I have always ripped engines apart and put the bits together again. I love to see an immediate improvement.

Troubleshooting was for me

After finishing my degree I loafed about for six
months before I was pressurised into taking a job.
This guy rang me up, having got my name off the
PER register. I suggested we meet at 1 o'clock and
he said: 'Make it 2 o'clock. I'll be in the pub at
one.' That seemed the place for me. I became the
chief and only chemist at Mercury Engineering
Company. I was cheap, basically. I worked for a
special guy. He was a magic man. Such charisma.
I would work for him any weekend he wanted. He
was a brilliant salesman with a lot of presence. As
long as I worked hard I was allowed my silly
periods.

It all made for a good working atmosphere. I've
got up to some amazing practical jokes. I need the
variety. In the late seventies I changed jobs and
joined Tapol. I've since travelled all round the world
with the company. Australia, New Zealand,
America, South Africa, the Middle East. That's
been a huge benefit. People now know me all over.
That's a mega spin off. I love meeting new people,
all these characters.

Becoming an agent of change

In mid 1984 I was appointed Tapol's Development
Manager. I wasn't expecting it at all. In fact I didn't
see myself as a manager at the time. Our Development Group was formed to get new products out
so as to improve our margins. The industry had
matured, margins had been falling, and we needed
to do something about it. We have to overcome
the attitude that big plants is where it's all at. Oil
stations. Power plants. That's the macho end. It's
at the small end, though, where you can afford
to make the cock ups.

You can't go to a big corporation and ask them
to try something risky and new. There could be
£2 billion at stake. On the other hand, if something

works with a little plant, you can always upgrade. We have to respond better to our customer needs, worldwide. If a customer says he needs so much, and will pay so much, we should be prepared to stick a plant in, run it, and provide an ongoing service. We should be flogging a service, the whole package. After all we're the only bastards who can do it.

Towards the management of change

I guess by now, as I enter my thirties, I'm just about beginning to see myself as a manager, but as a manager of change. I still like fixing things but now I get an extra kick out of getting a team spirit together. It's a different kind of fixing. I'd never have realised that I could get such satisfaction out of sorting out a team of people, getting people to do things on their own initiative.

I love generating ideas, particularly with other people. I don't like books, particularly the heavy stuff, full of management jargon. I also don't like being told what to do. It frightens me when I see people plan their days, meticulously. I'm always looking for the unexpected. In fact I'm expected to be the outrageous one at our management meetings. I hate processed people and totally predictable situations.

The spirit of freedom

I love eccentrics. I guess you'd see controlled anarchy around here. You need some people to do the donkey work, yet I want people to say 'There's another way of doing things'. I bring graduates in here when they're fresh, before they're tarnished. I make sure this is not an ivory tower. After a while we send them out of here, to get into sales.

We've had a lot of young characters through here. We have to make sure that they all have some place to go where they can be themselves. Perhaps one day people will come to see me as the 'free spirit' around the place, and I'll set some kind of example for them.

Who RECRUITS change agents?

There is a potentially rich crop of change agents in Great Britain. However, because you change agents are characteristically freedom-loving souls, like Steve Shirley, you are often put off the large and established organisations. You either choose to remain independent freelancers or else join the more flexible design groups, advertising agencies, computer software houses or management consultancy groups.

Should you choose to join a large corporation, like Tom Preen, you are often kept well away from the corridors of power so as not to disrupt things – unless an enlightened fellow like Don Rowlands recognises your potential. This conventional behaviour turns into self-fulfilling prophecy in that prospective change agents might not become sufficiently mature or 'politically streetwise' to develop and implement desirable changes.

However, in recent years there has been a welcome rise to power of designers and electronics experts, many of whom are beginning to act in such a change-making capacity. They are adding weight and strength to the opportunities for change being opened up every day by changes in lifestyles and by the emerging communications technologies.

How should companies REWARD change agents?

You agents of change, by definition, want to be free to make the sorts of changes you consider appropriate. Such adaptations in products and processes, systems and procedures often cut across conventional functions. As a result you want to be able to move across functional boundaries freely, and constantly, as Tom Preen has done.

As a change agent you seek continuing mental stimulus. If you do not feel you are learning and developing yourself you will seek a change. Bureaucratic, unadaptive organisations can be particularly stifling for you in that respect. Your primary motivation is neither financial reward nor formal promotion but variety of experience and opportunity for self-expression.

How do you DEVELOP yourself as an agent of change?

Characteristically you start out in organisational life as a professionally qualified designer, computer programmer, training officer, or technologist. In your early years you may be called in as a troubleshooter, to investigate problems and opportunities of a technical, commercial and human nature. You will typically be involved in a variety of time-bound tasks and projects. Your 'dream' is to be free to be yourself.

As you develop, having attended specific courses, travelled around the company, and visited different locations, you can become a more knowledgeable agent of change able to take on more significant assignments. You will be called in not only to solve particular problems but to apply more generalisable solutions.

As you consolidate your position within a function, as Tom Preen has done in his thirties, you will be in a position to enter the ranks of functional management as a manager of change. Your need for variety and mental stimulus will be tempered by willingness to focus on longer-term problems and opportunities. Your own need for self-expression will be matched by your desire to help others express themselves within your functional area, be it in R&D – as with Tom Preen – marketing, management services or in management training.

Finally, as you mature, like Steve Shirley, your role will become more symbolic than practical, so that you become fully yourself in maturity. You then come to embody the spirit of freedom rather than continuing to rush mentally and physically from one project or product to another. In other words you will come to represent and even lead a particular cause, like 'shaping work around the individual' or 'giving people the freedom to pursue wild ideas', rather than solely managing a particular and adaptable function or project.

On your own, however, even with the support of entrepreneurs and animateurs, you will be unable to steer your company in the right direction. For all the intellectual thrust that you are able to provide, you lack the necessary stability, staying power, and sense of coherence to provide rounded leadership. That is where your counterpart comes in, the business leader.

Are you a LEADER?

By focusing too heavily on standardised principles of management some academics and practitioners have done the business world a disservice. Not only have they forced our would-be corporate entrepreneurs, animateurs, or change agents into an uncomfortable mould, but they have laid too much responsibility at conventional management's door.

They have obliged standardised managers to be all things to all people. They have also falsely placed the manager in an aggressively competitive mould. Rather it should be the entrepreneur, from an emotional standpoint, and the change agent from an intellectual one, who carry this responsibility.

As a conventional and general manager you need to be viewed as more of a heroine rather than as a hero. You are a co-ordinator, a conciliator, and a generalist rather than a competitor, a controller and a specialist. You are likely to have scored highest on category (d) in the spectral inventory.

As a business leader like John Harvey Jones, therefore, you are a more rational version of the animateur. You are a midwife, a steward, a nurturer, and a unifier. As a 'bureaucrat', in the best sense of the word, it is the qualities of impartiality, fairness, and justice which should mark you out rather than those of, say, regimentation and impersonality. As a prospective leader, like Bert Hammil, you are a conciliator or referee, a person of integrity who rises above the competitive fray.

BERT HAMMIL *MANAGER*
DIVISIONAL DIRECTOR

I think very few people know what they'd like to do when they leave school. So I guess you get into your chosen field by default. I didn't have any strong vocational wish to be an engineer. But it seemed to be a field, in my native Canada, in which there were good job prospects.

Professional and management trainee

So I did a four-year degree in civil engineering at Toronto University. After graduation I took up a position with the regional authority in hydraulic and structural design. I subsequently spent two years with a consulting firm applying my newly acquired expertise to hydraulogical surveys. One of our clients was Brill Construction (Canada).

My opportunities for advancement had seemed limited within the consulting firm, so I looked outside. It was an interesting experience working for Brill, but they had two entrenched partners and there were no long term prospects.

So I joined Tapol at the age of 25. At the time it was basically an environmental engineering company with a staff of thirty. I started off doing project engineering and became steadily and increasingly more involved in management.

Functional management

I had joined Tapol (Canada) in 1963 and two years later was on the Board. I combined my management function, primarily on the technical side, with contracting activities. Since 1963 the company has grown from 30 to 100 people. Its activity has widened from predominantly pollution control equipment to generalised scientific instrumentation.

Fortunately, concurrent with these developments, the Canadian government embarked on a number of 'think big' projects. They were dreamt up to decrease our dependence on imported petro-chemically based products for both strategic and economic reasons. I was the one who got involved in representing ourselves all over the world.

Becoming an executive

My overseas experience proved invaluable. I was approached by Rob, a few months ago, to join him at Hydra's headquarters. He is wanting to make the company more international. We've tended, in recent years, to build up autonomous operating units, in some cases even competing with one another. We need to be able now to structure cooperation.

We've got to create an environment that will lead the operating companies in the right direction. We need to offer an international and broadened perspective. I'm looking at ways in which we can manage interdependence via international contracts.

Providing leadership

Just last week I was appointed chief executive of our environmental engineering division in the UK. There's a tremendous spirit there, deep down, but it needs channelling. The business is undergoing rapid change and they need a leader with a long-term perspective. I hope I can rise to the challenge, and make the contribution that is required of me.

Who recruits potential LEADERS?

The systematic recruitment of managers has been going on for the past two decades, both from the business schools and from within the managed organisations themselves. There are two remaining problems, though, to be addressed.

Firstly, prospective leaders have been traditionally recruited from the ranks of men rather than women. Although this is rapidly changing, particularly in the retailing sector and in the personnel function, there is still a long way to go before equality of opportunity becomes a reality.

Secondly, conventional management, at least outside Japan, is seldom seen in the decidedly 'feminine' light that we have cast for it. Although most progressive companies are now calling for more generalists, it is seldom realised that women are often able to resist the temptation to specialise better than men.

Once company recruiters begin to lay more stress on the co-ordinating, harmonising and integrative role that executives should play we might well find different sorts of people coming forward for leadership posts.

How do you REWARD potential leaders?

Sophisticated schemes have already been developed for rewarding executives. For it is the potential leaders amongst you who particularly appreciate the increasing authority and responsibility, as well as the enhanced status and remuneration, that go with conventional job promotion.

Moreover, once it is recognised that it is only executive types who seek that particular form of remuneration, there will be less pressure, within the organisation, for a single line of promotion. The organisational ladder – whether functionally, sectorally or territorially based – should serve only the hierarchically inclined amongst us. At the moment our one-dimensional orientation leads to unnecessary overcrowding.

How do you DEVELOP towards leadership?

The formal, credential-based training programmes run by business and management schools are geared towards the typically 'brainy' executive. Each business discipline has body of knowledge that underlies it – untainted by messy reality.

However, where the greatest difficulty is still found is in schooling individuals for a more generalist role. For it is in fact the school of working life which offers the best form of training for such general abilities. In your younger years you are likely to enter this 'school' as a trainee manager. Your 'dream' is to serve society.

It may well be, thereafter, that progressively more challenging and varied job assignments, coupled with an action learning approach, provide the best of both worlds of practice and theory. Within such action learning groups, and live projects, scope is provided for design and implementation, as well as for objective knowledge and subjective insight. Ultimately, however, it is the responsibility and authority that a general management role carry that offer the best grounds for consolidation.

To develop from a general manager to a business executive on the board, requires, as Bert Hammil found, exposure to a wide range of business disciplines, situations, problems and opportunities. It also requires, amongst ordinary management mortals, the kind of wisdom, empathy and perspective that come with age and experience.

As you enter midlife and maturity you may be able to provide that extra amount of authority and conviction that come with depth as well as breadth of perspective. Your determination to make a fundamental contribution to society will transform yourself and the spirit of leadership that you have now built up. Together with your aggressive counterparts, the agents of change, you will be in position to advance your organisation's cause fundamentally.

Between the two of you, as change agent and as leader, you establish a professionally managed organisation. While the one designs and implements specialised systems and methods the other devises and maintains an overall business strategy and organisation structure.

However, only a certain proportion of you are suited to developing along this path of rational management. Too often you are led to believe that, should you not be an entrepreneur, then staff or line management are the only paths open to you.

Most of us feel reasonably familiar with such business individualities as entrepreneur, change agent and leader, even if the animateur remains a little remote from our everyday awareness.

The flexible change agent and authoritative leader in fact take us to the limits of conventional wisdom within a managed organisation. We resist the attempt to understand the Japanese because their particular brand of adaptability and harmony falls beyond our common business consciousness.

However, as 'Japan Inc' takes the business world ever more by storm we shall eventually be obliged to wake up to one or two further varieties of 'intrapreneur', more Eastern than Western in character. In fact this myopic viewpoint has also been largely responsible for the management plateau at midlife.

****

238 *Enterprise Development*

****
The New Designer or Enabler
****

The role of 'enabler' has been much underplayed within
our organisations, and in fact relegated to a fringe position
within the training and development function. The trouble
is that this conventionally soft character has lacked a hard
counterpart.

Fortunately, however, in the 1980s, the design function
– at least in Great Britain – has risen to prominence. As
a result I have adopted the term 'new designer' to replace
the enabler as an intrapreneur of the fifth kind. As an enabler
you have a particular affinity for harmony and interdependence amongst people and things. You are at home within
a 'mature' organisation whose prime focus is on development.

Are you a prospective ENABLER 'NEW DESIGNER'?

Interestingly enough I suspect that the Japanese have
developed a hard counterpart to the enabler, or new designer,
and this eighth intrapreneur may be called an 'adaptor'. But
because he remains largely invisible to Western eyes I have
chosen to leave him out.

Harmony and coherence are particular qualities that the
Japanese, over and above any other contemporary business
nation, have brought to corporate life. The force that binds
is not the personality of the animateur nor the generality
of the manager but the sensitivity of the enabler (or 'new
designer').

As a new designer like Mary Quant, you have an acute
appreciation of subtlety and balance, amongst products and
markets as well as people and organisations. Your approach
is individually and collaboratively oriented rather than
personality-based and competitive. This applies in person-to-
person, business-to-business, supplier-to-customer and
corporate-to-government dealings.

You therefore enable people and organisations, as Jim
Squires is doing, or products and markets, as Mary Quant

is doing, to realise their unique identity and potential. You achieve this by recognising and harnessing opportunities for synergy across space and time. You recognise that true individuality is acquired through genuine interdependence, and vice versa.

In the same way, as you grow and develop as an intrapreneur, you imbibe qualities from others who are different from yourself. Thus Jim Squires is making it his business to ensure that he is not isolated within a personnel enclave.

JIM SQUIRES   *ENABLER* PERSONNEL MANAGER

At the age of 11 I went to grammar school, which I didn't enjoy at all. By the time I reached my fifth year I began to understand why. All the rules and regulations related to the past rather than to the present or future. As I got into the sixth form I realised that the school was about preparing candidates for Oxbridge. That was the be-all and the end-all of our education.

The art and science of management

I didn't fit the conventional system because I wanted to do management studies. I wanted to discover what really made managers tick. I went on to read Business Studies at Enfield College of Technology, and that was really great. The subjects at last had some meaning.

In my third year, at College, Jean and I got married. At that stage of my life I thought I'd want to lecture at an F.E. College. An opportunity came up for a training placement in industry, and subsequently a job, with a Scandinavian-based firm. It was terrific. Gradually I developed knowledge and skill in all aspects of personnel management.

Designing training programmes

In the last few months of my job I'd become involved in management succession planning. That kind of hooked me. I was then offered a job by Mirak Industries as Management Development Officer. By then I'd come to enjoy working with managers on their problems. At my Scandinavian company in the Midlands all the training programmes had been rigidly prescribed. My approach to management development was more personal, more intensive and, where possible, more individually oriented.

Working for Mirak was quite a change. There were 8000 people on one site. The training manager there was building up a team. I got involved in lots of things. Action-centred leadership. Supervisor training. Closed-circuit TV. We also spent a lot of time working with the shop floor. Just before I left we were involved with a programme on organisational development.

However, in my heart of hearts, I knew we couldn't succeed. I felt there were just too many layers of authority. I became very aware of the overly extensive span of control. So I left Mirak and joined Hydra.

Enabling development

Two years ago I started using assessment centre techniques to find out people's attitudes and competencies. Among the competencies we were trying to assess were 'proactivity' and 'goal setting'. We discovered, to our increasing consternation, that we had few 'proactives'. Then Rob Hurst came on the scene. He began to express the same concern over the lack of proactivity, albeit in his own, different words. The question that arose was – how could we make the organisation more enterprising? One response was an 'intrapreneurship' programme.

You see, I don't see my role as a conventional personnel manager. The average personnel manager is very remote from the mainstream of the business. I see myself as part of a management team here. We have already been considering how we want to be seen within and without the company, and why such an umbrella organisation failed in the past. We need to operate as a complementary group of individuals. In fact I'm finding that people here don't know my job title. The secretaries don't see me as a straight personnel man. Any one of us could be brought in, for support, for almost anything.

I see myself, then, doing much more significant and varied boundary crossing than ever before. I see people moving in and out of corporate head-quarters as part of their development. I am constantly involved, here, in linking people, problems and opportunities, and sharing them all around. Talking to people externally is another kind of boundary crossing that helps me to keep my sanity.

The developmental spirit

Hydra, finally, also needs to evolve internationally. I'd like to feel there'll be enough time for me to get to know the other businesses, all over the globe, so that I'll be able to develop potential on a world-wide basis. Who knows, as we develop our combined capability across R&D, organisation and business development – we may come to release the full spirit of development in this country.

Who RECRUITS enablers/new designers?

The role of the enabler has only become widely recognised in the areas of management and organisation development. As someone who can recognise and develop human potential you will often have a background in social psychology or in industrial design. So you can indeed be recruited via conventional graduate channels.

I have deliberately broadened the term 'enabler's' usage to include industrial designers who are adept at recognising and developing the potential of new products, materials and technologies in fulfilling market needs. As design and tech-nology become an integral part of business development so the scope for recruiting the design-based enabler increases.

Finally, fertile ground for enabling recruits lies with the functional specialist or manager who has reached midlife, and who needs to broaden out rather than deepen his or her involvement with management. To the extent that such individuals could be redirected at mid-career so the infamous plateauing of management could be stemmed.

Particularly if you scored highest in category (c) in the spectral inventory – whether you are a technologist, a designer or a functional manager – you should be positioning yourself within a broadly based development role.

How can you be REWARDED as an enabler or 'new designer'?

As an enabler you feel rewarded when you can see development – of people, of products, of businesses or of landscapes – arising before you. You hate to see physical or human potential go to waste.

You need to combine with other people, as Mary Quant and Jim Squires have done, often outside your own organisation, so as to enable change and evolution to take place. As a result you find opportunities to step outside the confines of your particular department or company most rewarding, particularly if you can then create some joint venture that is of mutual benefit.

Conventional salaries, derived from a single source, run counter to your interest in building up a combination, of linked economic, personal and social benefits. You would rather, over time, build up a composite reward package, made up of a number of corporate constituents, than be limited to a single source.

How can you DEVELOP as an enabler/new designer?

Enablers or 'new designers' – particularly amongst the older members of a company's staff – are the largest and, to my mind, the least exploited intrapreneurial resource. Your potential, often latent rather than actual, generally goes to waste because there are so few recognised channels for your deployment.

The best recognised of the currently available channels in a mature company are in R and D, and in people and organisation development. Emerging channels today include industrial design and community economic development. You are likely to enter one or the other as a natural or social scientist, or as a fine artist, in your youth. Your 'dream' is to enhance potential.

However, until the enabling path becomes recognised right across the functional board, it will remain − conventional designers perhaps excepted − largely a dead end. As an enabler, who is recognised at an early age, you can only consolidate your position if you are given opportunities to work in product, market, business, organisation or community design. Only in that way can you exercise, and develop, your distinctive competences in young adulthood.

It is also important to recognise that you are likely to follow a path that is neither linear nor bounded. It will tend to be diagonal and associative, like Mary Quant's picking up threads of involvement within and outside the organisation. To that extent the recent spate of joint ventures − whether technologically, commercially, or community based − is ideal for you, if you are allowed to round out your position as a broadly based enabler.

In your forties and fifties you may develop the breadth of interest, and the depth of conviction, to co-ordinate a major shift in the design and orientation of a business operation − based upon changing tastes and technologies. This is the stage Jim Squires is reaching in Hydra.

In order to achieve this you may have to bring together engineers, psychologists and marketeers within the company, and design and technology consultants from without. You become, at one and the same time, your ultimate self and the embodiment of the developmental spirit within the company.

As a broadly based enabler, then, you are responsible for the continued evolution of the particular organism, or organisation, in which you are based. In fact, in my book *The Global Business*[1] I refer to you as a 'corporate architect'.

For you link form and function, actual and potential, in a spirit of harmony and interdependence.

So much for the enabler or new designer, a much neglected intrapreneur within conventional organisations. Like Mary Quant or Jim Squires she or he holds ultimate responsibility for the evolution of their organisation, including its products and people. Their counterpart, perhaps an adaptor, I have not examined. But there is one last pair of intrapreneurs, and that is the adventurer and the innovator.

****

```
******************************
```
Adventurer and Innovator
```
******************************
```

The most basic element of business life is not money, nor is it people; it is energy. It is the adventurer who releases raw energy, in its purest form, and it is the genuine innovator who is able to create new energy forms. The most highly evolved corporations, like the multinational Bank of Commerce and Credit, will take particular note of these last two intrapreneurs.

There is a strange bond between the adventurer, compelled to risk life and limb, and the innovator, compelled to devote his whole life and livelihood to the realisation of his dream. While the one ventures into the physical unknown, the other enters a technical, artistic or social void. Both, like Roddick and Conran, are obsessive in their intrapreneurial pursuits.

Are you an ADVENTURER?

Adventurers have been part of the British culture for centuries Francis Drake, Brunel, T.E. Lawrence, and now Anita Roddick (not to mention Richard Branson and Ian Botham), are all part of that adventurous heritage. All have ventured into far-flung territories, risking life and limb as they pursued their political, business or social missions.

With the advent of a more leisure-oriented society, in which health and fitness have an increasing part to play, the role of adventurer is creeping ever more strongly into business. If you scored highest in category (a) in the spectral inventory, like Dick Knowles, you may be one.

DICK KNOWLES   *ADVENTURER*
GENERAL MANAGER, PURETEK

I trained initially as an aeronautics engineer. I completed my training in 1944 when I volunteered for the Navy. I got involved in night flying and generally enjoyed life. Soon after that I started flying the Sea Vampire, flying jets off small carrier decks. Then my flying career was cut short. My eyesight was not that good and I failed the medical. I decided that I had to face up to reality and get out.

I did something unusual at the time. I put a catchy advert in the aeronautics press. I said I was interested in opportunity and adventure. I wanted to make an impact. I got replies, aside from the inevitable life assurance companies, from Baker Perkins and from Tapol. Tapol offered me a position in overseas sales. I was 25 and I jumped at it. It was 1951.

Young adventurer

By 1955, though, the company considered me reliable enough to go off on my own. So began my travels abroad. Nigeria, Poland, East Germany, Russia. In those days it took $2\frac{1}{2}$ days to get to Nigeria, even by plane. To get to East Germany I had to walk through Checkpoint Charlie and then take another plane on the other side. I was something of a lamb sent to slaughter. But I persevered. I became Deputy Export Manager, Export Manager and then Manager of our business unit.

Activating sales

The company anyway decided to bring in a firm of management consultants. They recommended that domestic and overseas sales be amalgamated. I was 42 at the time, undergoing my first male menopause. I decided that export sales were too important for me to let go. So I left Tapol and came over to a sister company, Puretek, where I became Managing Director, with a special interest in the exporting side.

I find selling challenging and I don't recognise when I'm beaten. You have to decide what's dead and alive, and then follow through. When you're moving into unknown territories, and you can't visualise the situation, you may also need a bit of courage. With our PMF product line we're inevitably dealing in developing and often precarious markets, like Iraq and Iran. But I get my real satisfaction now, and have done for the past ten years, not out of selling myself, but out of galvanising my sales force into action.

The spirit of adventure

I am 62 by now, and well into maturity. I haven't lost my zest for travel, though I'm beginning to get different things out of it.

I've travelled to 58 countries – Australia, New Zealand, Indonesia, Malaysia, Pakistan, Ghana, Nigeria, Libya, the Gulf States, France, Spain, Norway included. Next week I'm off to Spain and then, probably, to Teheran.

When I go to these places, especially now, I make it my business to get to know the country. In Libya I hire a car for myself and drive off to see the Roman ruins. In Nigeria I've spent weeks in small villages. There's something about Africa, there's also something about India. No wonder the British went out to these countries. It wasn't only the money. It's the spirit of adventure.

Do companies RECRUIT adventurers?

As companies spread their international wings, particularly in the remoter parts of our planet, so the call for the adventurer is increasingly heard. As research take us up into outer space and down into the depths of the oceans, this demand for adventurers is likely to grow. The mercenary or merchant adventurer of old is being replaced by a more educated business adventurer of the 1980s and 1990s.

At the same time, as the pressures of competitive business mount, the demand for adventure training, for adventure holidays, and the like, increases. Work hard, play hard becomes both a desire and a psychological necessity.

The particular parts of a business organisation that are likely to be most interested in you, as an adventurer, are export sales, publicity and promotions, research and exploration, and the more physically hazardous production operations, especially in mining and agriculture.

How are you REWARDED, as an adventurer?

Adventurers, like Anita Roddick, Richard Branson, and Dick Knowles, need to keep constantly on the move. If they are not physically active they feel no sense of achievement.

So as an adventurer you have physical challenges to surmount, like Branson's attempt to cross the Atlantic in a hot air balloon, and Roddick's desire to keep picking up skin and hair-care recipes from all over the world.

Equally, you may seek comfort in good food and wine, in exercise and massage, in sunny beaches on the Caribbean, or in pleasurable sporting holidays.

How do you DEVELOP as an adventurer?

In your youth you may come across as an action man or woman. Like Dick Knowles, you may have sold to more countries than anyone else in your company, by footslogging around the world.

In young adulthood, you become more visible in the company as a whole, as an adventurer. Like Richard Branson you are physically 'on show' so as to publicise your product and your business.

In midlife, as Dick Knowles is doing, you become less involved in your own physical accomplishments, and more in activating others, in sales or on exploration, through coaching or by intensive rather than extensive 'mentorial' example.

Finally, in your fifties and sixties, as is beginning to happen with Dick Knowles, as you actualise your true self, you come to embody the spirit of adventure, by broadening the base of your physical accomplishments. Instead of leading from the front you inspire from up above, by, for example, transforming a physical environment rather than keeping yourself physically on the go. Interestingly enough Anita Roddick has very recently begun to show a more active interest in achieving this, through 'Greenpeace'.

As you develop towards maturity, in fact, you come close to the role of innovator, your counterpart.

Are you a prospective INNOVATOR?

Broadly based innovators, as opposed to the purely technical variety, are few and far between in our society, and they are more visible in politics – Disraeli, Gandhi, Luther King – than in business.

Yet this was not always the case. Brunel and Stephenson in the railways, Nobel and Mond in the chemical industry – just to mention four – were powerful innovators of yesteryear. Perhaps the best example of such an intrapreneur today, at least in Great Britain, is Terence Conran. If you see yourself as such a person, and you are honest with yourself, you will have topped the spectral inventory with category (b).

So fully fledged innovators, like one or two of you, are about. It is just that it may take a lifetime for you to realise your dream, and the realisation usually comes later in life rather than sooner. At a young age we can usually only identify the seeds of our vision, rather than the ripening fruit. Rob Hurst of Hydron, who is still in his forties, in that respect has some way to go.

ROB HURST   *INNOVATOR*
CHIEF EXECUTIVE

My father worked as a shop assistant all his adult life and my mother was a nurse. We lived in Bradford and struggled to make ends meet. I felt that there had to be more to life than that. I went to the local tech and left school with six 'O'levels, being fortunate in having a maths master at school who took a shine to me. So maths became my favourite subject. In my spare time I loved tinkering about with old cars and discovering for myself how things mechanical worked.

I ended up as a student apprentice at what was to become the Central Electricity Generating Board. I did a five-year apprenticeship there while studying part-time at the local technical college. Then I had my first really lucky break.

Maverick inventor

The CEGB at the time were offering, in association with the trade unions, a scholarship for people with a deprived educational background. I won it. I went off to do my PhD at Sheffield University. The subject of my research was combustion. At the time I was completely motivated by the technology and had no interest whatsoever in management.

My superviser was an oddball, a maverick inventor. He allowed me to dream up my own project and then to go ahead and do the work, my own way. Having been a student apprentice, I could actually weld and fit, so I was streets ahead of the more academic students. I completed my PhD in chemical engineering after three years, at the age of 27. By then I had a wife and three small children to support, so I abandoned the creative freedom of academic life, with some reluctance.

The challenge and responsibility of innovation

So we moved to London and I joined the design team at the CEGB. I was the appointed combustion expert.

As I turned thirty something fundamental began to dawn on me. I realised that unless you got involved on the management side you would never really get to grips with the overall design concept, that is with the overall process of innovation. In fact, I was beginning to get very frustrated. As a specialist engineer you could add your twopence-worth to a management meeting, and that was that. There had to be more exciting places to be than in that of a quiet specialist. It was around then that I was approached by Tapol.

I decided to join them and was put on site for the first twelve months, as a commision engineer on the power station. After that initial grounding I was appointed Technical Manager. I had joined, for the first time in my life, the ranks of management. I welcomed the responsibility involved. As I sorted out one contract after another I acquired a reputation for being able to resolve troubled contracts, both on the technical and commercial sides.

I approached things from first principles, tackling situations as they were rather than as I'd like them to have been. So I was given overall responsibility for contracts. I also discovered that I loved being in charge.

Then came my third big stroke of luck. The Hydra top management was being restructured and a vacancy came up at the head of Tapol. Tapol was a subsidiary of the Hydra Group. I was given the top job at Tapol at 37.

Broadening my vision

I took over the whole of the Hydra Group just over a year ago, and now face a wide variety of fresh challenges. At the moment our companies are too fragmented. We could end up, if we're not careful, with a whole lot of companies with which we can do nothing but slash overheads. Instead I'm working on a plan to integrate our widely spread operations on a truly international basis.

That will mean a change not only in the structure but also in the culture of this place. We shall have to work much more consciously as a team, acknowledging our interdependence with on another. Like our geographical spread, our reserach and development has become too fragmented. We need to establish one or two centres of technical excellence. We have to create an environment within which one or two genuine innovators can prosper. I have to provide the vision to inspire our technological effort.

Towards a spirit of creativity

If I look at my own journey through life, with the benefit of hindsight, I can now see how I pulled myself up by my own bootstraps in my teens and twenties, and then took on more and more challenges and responsibilities as I grew older.

In my late thirties and forties I was to broaden my scope, from research to implementation, from technology to management, from national to international, and from Tapol to the Hydra Group. Now my task must be to integrate this diversity, by creating a climate in which enterprise, innovation and sheer difference can combine and flourish.

In my fifties, perhaps, I might even embody, dare I say, the spirit of creativity that is needed not only in Hydra but also in the engineering-based companies in Great Britain as a whole.

Who recruits INNOVATORS?

Innovators as described above are like gold dust. Unfortunately the popular business press brackets innovators and entrepreneurs together as if they were the same breed. This is not strictly true. You innovators are to be found amongst the ranks of highly imaginative artists or scientists. If our corporations can succeed in attracting these creative technologists and designers they will do both you and themselves a great service.

In order to attract you a company will have to project its image in brilliantly imaginative terms. Companies, rather than being mere patrons of the arts, would need to create and project their own art forms, as Conrad is currently doing through his design group. Innovation becomes central rather than peripheral to your company's existence – something to which Rob Hurst is aspiring.

How do you reward INNOVATORS?

You innovators gain your ultimate satisfaction from seeing your dreams turned into reality. In other words the far-reaching potential of your technical, artistic or social imaginations needs to be recognised, converted into a product or service, furnished with adequate resources, adapted to changing conditions and circumstances, and warmly accepted by people inside and outside the organisation.

To the extent, then, that your far-reaching idea was turned into reality you would feel duly rewarded. You might then see your creative idea spiral upwards and outwards like nuclear fission, like what is happening to Conran today. Landmarks along the road to transformation would be scientific or design breakthroughs, together with the flashes of inspiration that served to achieve them.

Ultimately you have no direct interest in progression along a career ladder. Your own progressive spiral, technologically or socially based, serves to elevate you from the bottom to a top which – in association with many others – is of your own making. In business terms you can but create your own products and markets.

How do you DEVELOP as an innovator?

The point about you, as an innovator, is that you reach your prime in maturity, that is from your late forties onwards. Unfortunately many an innovator never realises his or her ultimate vision because he is not encouraged to follow a natural line of development.

In your youth you need to explore, to experiment, to risk your personal resources or identity in a new invention. Travel into the physically, economically, or psychologically unknown is therefore a natural feature of healthy, youthful development. This is certainly reflected in Terence Conran's youth and, to a lesser extent, in Rob Hurst's.

For the young adult, authority and responsibility now come naturally to the developing innovator. Thus the freewheeling inventor needs to come to grips with the problems of managing innovation – from idea generation to commercialisation. Whereas the twenties are therefore a time for enterprise, the thirties are the prime time for structured organisation.

Midlife is the time to listen to your heart first and your head second. As a technological innovator you need to broaden your social awareness, becoming a true visionary. Thus Conran becomes more interested in a social revolution than in a particular product line. Rob Hurst begins to envisage a new role for engineering in our society.

Finally, if you have successfully undergone life's transitions, as a mature individual you are ready to tap the very core of your own being, your spirit of creativity. In so doing you also connect yourself with the core of your company's being. The relationship between the one and the other is a particularly powerful one, resulting in a fully developed vision. This is, interestingly enough, more apparent in the case of Anita Roddick and Bodyshop than for Conran and Storehouse.

The intrapreneurial paths of adventurer and innovator are somewhat more visible than those of enabler and adaptor, but as yet only barely accommodated in conventional organisations. Technological innovators and rugged adventurers are generally relegated to the mature business periphery, even though it is acknowledged that their role has been indispensable.

Without Alfred Nobel there would have been no ICI; without George Eastman there would have been no Kodak; without Masaru Ibuka there would have been no Sony. Yet our commercial memories are short. All too quickly we lose sight of our real energy source, both in its conception and in its continued activation. Therein lies the creative nucleus, the 'soul' of the business, and its physical outcome.

****

Developing your business individuality

In conclusion, you might say that there are eight intrapreneurial paths, seven of which have been made visible to us in this book. Each path makes its way through four stages of development, interspersed with transitional phases.

In realising your business individuality, you will probably be best suited to forge, or to follow, one or other of these. In the process you will explore in your youth, consolidate in adulthood, renew yourself in midlife, and become your ultimate, and intrapreneurial self in maturity.

Table 14.1
Developing your business individuality

EXPLORATION (youth)	CONSOLIDATION (adulthood)	RENEWAL (midlife)	INDIVIDUATION (maturity)
Action Man	*Adventurer*	Activator	Spirit of Adventure
Craftsman	Skilled Operator	*Animateur*	Community Spirit
Troubleshooter	*Change Agent*	Manager of Change	Free Spirit
Salesman	*Entrepreneur*	Business Developer	Enterprise Spirit
Trainee Manager	Functional Manager	Business Executive	*Spirit of Leadership*
Artist/ Scientist	Designer	*Enabler*	Spirit of Development
Inventor	*Innovator*	Visionary	Creative Spirit

At this point very few 'intraprises' have structured themselves to accommodate such individuality. However, ICI, British Rail, Rio Tinto and Eastern Highlands Tea Estates, as well as our British-based engineering company, have made a start. Thousands of individuals, particularly women, are now beginning to see themselves as adventurers, animateurs, change agents, entrepreneurs, leaders, enablers and innovators rather than as one-dimensional managers or employees.

Reference

1 Lessem, R., *The Global Business*, Prentice-Hall, 1987.